I0532354

# FORMULATION YOU

*Brandon Adalid*

For more information, email me at badalidlmu@gmail.com

A guide to give readers sustainable strategies and thought processes in order to live, function, and perform at the most optimal level no matter what age an individual is.

Dedicated to everyone committing themselves to be better in mind, body, and spirit so that they will become beacons of hope and inspiration to their own inner circle of people.

Dedicated to coachable, yearning, open-minded lifelong learners.

Dedicated to everyone who has the courage to step into their personalized power of light, turn their mess into a message, and be the person they are truly meant to be.

Dedicated to all of those who enjoy and appreciate the gift of kinesthetic body movement.

To Ben and Josie, the best set of grandparents
a little boy can ask for!

# CONTENTS

# PREFACE

Our journeys in life differ from one person to the next. Pathways, successes, and failures are all present in these journeys, but the one common denominator in these processes are the adversities we all face. Without a doubt, life challenges have a diverse range of magnitudes, scopes, categories, and modalities.

The major challenge that affected my life is my well-being and overall health. This obstacle is never ending, and I deal with the notion of attempting to be better as each day goes by in my life. Poor health is an issue with many people nowadays and has escalated over the years.

The motivating reason why I wrote this book is to put my story of health transformation on display to give readers the positive possibilities and results they want to attain. I felt compelled to put my story out there for others to draw inspiration from, and I thought it would be a disservice upon my livelihood if I did not act upon this matter.

I hope the material resonates with you so you can take radical responsibility and massive action for yourself and be an inspirational figure within your own environment. There is this misconception and interpretation on what health is truly about, and I am on a mission to help people realize that health and wellness is a long-term commitment of love for yourself. It is a skill-building process you will have to build on your own so you can give yourself grace within this journey. You need to attain an infinite-mind attitude within this mission.

People will ask, "Who are you to write such a book?" I am a former youth physical education teacher and athletics coach who has a high passion for human movement, tactics to implement on a health journey, and cooking. I am not an expert on nutrition, athletic training, or functional holistic medicine! I do, however, have a vested interest in those categories and have picked up valuable lessons in those areas over the course of time. I am a lifelong learner and always eager and inquisitive with anything that has to do with the human body. I am simply one individual soul who made changes and took drastic actions to continually attain extraordinary fulfillment in health and wellness.

I will introduce my personal transformation—what I went through—and show my progression pictures at the end of this introductory portion. The book will then be broken down into three sections where I will address thought processes, strategies, personal experiences, and life hacks you can immediately incorporate into your daily lives in each.

Part I will talk about mentality and mindset. Here I place an emphasis on how to properly think about your transformation. I will give tips on how to conduct yourself as a person and stress the relevance of daily preparation, perception of others, progression in terms of avoiding the comparison game, and reception of judgment and praise from your inner circle.

Part II of the book will delve into the spiritual/emotional phase of a transformation. I will introduce the idea of vindictive intentions and how that plays an intricate role on attaining personal goals. I will touch base upon how the people in your life can be a positive or negative influence toward you and how you coordinate yourself around those factors. I will mention the notion of having an "attitude of gratitude," which speaks volumes on how people will feel about you and most importantly how you will feel about yourself.

Part III is the physical side of the transformation. In this final section, you will be informed on strategies regarding food consumption, exercise, hydration, and manageable adaptations you can insinuate so you can position yourself into a better, healthier lifestyle.

In the end of the book, we will bring everything together and elaborate why all three components are essential to attaining a healthy, well-balanced lifestyle and achieving the ultimate formula of "you."

Upon the completion of reading this book, my hope is for you to recognize the addressed principles and strategies and take ownership on those ideas and customize them to make it yours! We are all different, and not everything I state in this book will work for everyone. However, if I can make the slightest impact on one of you, it would mean so much to me because a positive difference is being made.

# INTRODUCTION

The roots of my wellness journey began when I was in high school where, at the time, I was told by many of my classmates to play football. It was here where I gained the athletes mentality where we as a team had to train for something. That "something" obviously was the football season ahead. I gained a lot of exercise perspectives on playing high school football! Physical intensity was the main principle that stuck with me even to this day. It was truly one of the first characteristics I learned about health and wellness.

In late 1999, I was well into college and football was over. There was no more frequency or intensity on that training, which then resulted with me tipping the scales at 320 pounds, my heaviest weight. So, I decided to tackle a health transformation head-on, the only way I knew at the time. I lost substantial weight and was proud of my personal progress. I felt so inspired, I went and attained a second bachelor's degree and a certified teaching credential in 2002 so I could teach PE (physical education) to youth students in promoting the importance of human movement.

I spent hours upon hours in the gym working so hard that I felt sore afterward. I was in this "no pain no gain" mindset. I was in the state of trying to "out-gym" my fork, spoon, and knife. I spent anywhere from two to three hours per session going four times a week. But the regimen that I was on was not at all sustainable. In lieu of that, I ended up gaining most of that weight back within a few years. The irony here is I was teaching physical education traits to kids, but in turn, I was not feeling as healthy that I wanted to be.

Over time, my weight fluctuated; there were periods where if I restricted myself with certain fatty/sugary foods, my weight went down a bit, but in due time it went back up. As I reached my mid-thirties, I decided to give the health transformation another try. This time around, I got involved with distance running. I had a better sense on how to eat, but deep down, it still felt like I was not where I was supposed to be. I ran miles upon miles to train for 10K and half marathon races. There was a time where I racked five half marathon races in eighteen months. I was in a different time, at an older age, but I was still in an unsustainable regimen. I was in the state of trying to "outrun" my fork, spoon, and knife.

Before that fifth half marathon race, my body gave way. I got injured in April, and the race was set to go in June. I could not train at the intensity or frequency I was accustomed. June came around, the race entrance fee was non-refundable, and my hotel accommodations were already set. My intention on race day was to show up for the race and as soon as my timing chip crossed the starting line, I would seek out one of the race officials and withdraw from the event. But who was I kidding? I was engulfed in that energetic environment with 20,000 people hyped, amped and ready to run. Adrenaline took over, and all of the sudden, my leg injury did not feel as bad. Excitement unraveled everywhere at that start area and I felt the need to accomplish this challenge.

I completed that half marathon with a hampered left leg. It was an exhilarating proud moment, but on the flip side, I knew deep down my running days and running ways were over. I needed to find a way to change my healthy lifestyle around for the better without physically exhausting myself on the journey.

During that distance training, I got down to the lowest weight I have ever been. Consequently, I could not train the way I wanted to because of that leg injury, so within less than a year, all that weight snuck back onto my body yet again.

Things came to fruition in the school year of 2016–2017. This was consequently my last year in physical education and athletics. In a nutshell, I experienced the breakdown to get to my breakthrough. The toll of stress, high cortisol levels, and anxiety from being in education was eating away at my body. I ran into a string of health issues ranging from lower back pain and joint pain. Moreover, I underwent tests such as CT scans for blood clots and a colon cancer screening.

At that ER visit for the possible blood clot, my doctor said the reading was negative, which was great news, but then he asked me a question I will never forget. He said, "Brandon, are you under a lot of stress at work?" I answered with a yes. He then told me to monitor myself very carefully and said I had costochondritis, which is the inflammation of the chest wall in my torso area. This event was the eye-opening switch I needed so I could seek the most proper way to attain a life full of wellness, abundance, and vibrance.

I followed the doctors' orders in monitoring myself carefully, but what became compromised was my ability and intensity to the way I was teaching. I had to take a step back for the sake of my health. Deep down in my heart, it felt as though the profession had run its course. I had to get out of that education realm because I needed to fix *me*, so I finished teaching that school year knowing it was my last. It was a heartbreaking moment for me because I did not leave the profession on my own terms.

Regarding my physical health, I was sick and tired of being sick and tired, and moreover, enough was enough. In fact, enough was far too much! I decided to enroll in a results-oriented lifestyle wellness program that completely changed the way I viewed nutrition and exercise. The program taught me that transformations come from within the body and that this was going to be an infinite way of approaching health. The lifestyle program altered the pathway of my life for the better. Transformations are about the soul, heart, and mental aspects. I had to realize that I needed to be more intentional, more caring of myself, and more grateful. It was about celebrating small victories along the way while nourishing my body more efficiently. And these are characteristics all of which have nothing to do with losing weight, but at the same time, they have everything to do with losing weight.

Through this third go-around at a transformation, I am proud to say that I dropped a lot of visceral fat that was a detriment around my vital organs. What really astonished me after losing the pounds is how I started to gain weight after a year into the lifestyle program. However, it was weight stemming from muscle development and a lot of strength gain. I am now in maintenance, hovering around a very healthy 215 to 225 pounds. This is not a finite situation! There is no "there"! You do not arrive at a final destination with health and wellness. There is only the everlasting journey of fulfillment that is filled with adaptations. Please note, I am always and forever will be a work in progress and am so proud to admit that I am perfectly imperfect.

# Part I:
# Mentality

*Impossible is just a big word thrown around by small men who find it easier to live in the world they've been given than to explore the power they have to change it. Impossible is not a fact. It's an opinion. Impossible is not a declaration. It's a dare. Impossible is potential. Impossible is temporary. Impossible is nothing.*

*—Muhammad Ali*

# Chapter 1

## *Mindset*

*Where focus goes, energy flows. And where energy flows,*
*whatever you're focusing on grows.*

—*Tony Robbins*

What may be the most powerful organ in our human bodies is our brain. How it functions, how it reacts, how it recalls, and how it triggers our execution, habits, and behaviors is unique compared to other species living in our planet. Our central nervous system is an astonishing tool. In addition to that, as human beings, we get the opportunity to verbally communicate with one another using many different dialects and languages. What a phenomenon! And if you think about it, we take for granted this ability to think and internalize then verbalize our expressions.

With this said, we think of others in our lives, which results in being generous and caring toward others. That is a fabulous attribute to have, but on the flip side of that, we need to have the mindfulness in caring and loving more to the most important person in life—and that is yourself. We give in extreme abundance to our loved ones, spouses, kids, career, and at the same time we juggle everything else in our daily lives. With that mentioned, the individual who gets the short end of the stick is you.

A question to ponder: If you are not at your best in mind, body, and spirit, then how can you portray your best self as a spouse/parent/child, a colleague, or as a mentor toward others? Without a doubt, there must be a give and take and a level of delegation between other people! There must be a compromise, a middle ground/meeting place of stability. And most people may question and disagree on what I am about to state, but there must be a level of selfishness on your behalf so you can become your most ideal self.

## Selfishness

There is a feeling of discomfort, guilt, and negativity when it comes to a person being deemed as selfish. However, to a certain extent, you will need to be selfish for the fact that you are taking massive action to personally develop yourself for the future horizon. It is completely different if you are being selfish at the expense of others. I am not delving into those scenarios because it has obvious self-explanatory outcomes (one party benefits from the gains, the other party suffers a loss from the intentions of the others). You will need to become selfish so you can showcase your best self, and there is nothing wrong with that.

In this scenario, you will reap the benefits of improving yourself with the result of becoming an inspiration. A few years ago, I was speaking to a coworker of mine, who is married with two kids.

She often confided in me about having low levels of energy and how much of a hardship it is to raise a family. I agree with her, and without a doubt, raising a family has many challenges and revolving variables. We would converse about her daily routine and how after work, her days get more hectic and busier as she heads out to pick up her kids from school and then come home to her family life. She then said something poignant to me that made an impact on me and made me realize how far I have come.

She asked, "What are you doing for yourself to attain so much energy? It seems like you gain more energy as the work shift progresses along!"

I then preceded to inform her about taking time for myself.

"But, Brandon, I do not have time to take for myself."

"This is where you need to be delegating to your spouse and say, 'I need to be a little selfish and take time for myself to be my best self for you and the kids.' There is indeed a sense of sacrifice if you need to take time for yourself to change and morph into the ideal self you want to be. Depending on circumstances and what is going on for you in these moments, sacrifices must be acknowledged and made for the priorities to come forth."

## Focus on Growth

Energy flow and focus can be a challenge when one wants to make a change to their well-being. The objective of undergoing a transformation can seem intimidating and daunting at the same time. When I get approached for advice and insights, I often say, "You are conducting yourself in a manner that you are already at your ideal transformed state (mentally, emotionally, and spiritually). You are acting and behaving as if you are your better self even though you have not made appropriate progression at the superficial level (appearance and weight loss)" I firmly believe in the power of the mind, because if you believe in the proper process for yourself, the manifestation will come toward you, and then it becomes you!

I created a daily morning movement routine where I walk to the end of the block of my residential street and back and just stand outside for a good two to three minutes in quiet. I then execute some basic flexibility exercises and have a glass of citrus water to start my day. That ten minutes alone on my morning routine can make the difference in your own life. Does it have to be those exact activities? No. Morning routines can be anything you want it to be, as long as you enjoy doing those processes.

The more energy and focus you devote to routines, the more it will transcend so that you can create other routines throughout your day. And the more manageable healthy routines you can create for yourself, the more you get to practice the behaviors involved with those intricacies. Moreover, the more consistent you execute the behaviors, the more they will transform into healthy beneficial habits. It is the habit forming that is relevant because once you can reach this threshold, things become second nature to you. It feels like a reflex, a natural part of you now.

# Nourishment

Our human bodies were made in a very practical manner where if we consume nutrient-dense foods, our bodies will perform better. I will touch base more deeply into nourishment from foods in Part III of the book. For the sake of my statement here, there is no shortcut around attaining energy.

Your mental state plays a major role on our relationship with food. The complexity of that comes into our human minds though. Executing the act of eating in a practical sense is the most difficult part. I am no brain expert or certified dietician by any means, but I have the experience to say that I at one point was addicted to soda pop, and the influx of sugar swayed my decision-making in my food consumption. It amazes me how our bodies crave those indulgent, palatable foods that are unctuously sweet and salty, which in turn makes your brain waves go haywire. You cannot perform or act at peak level if the food you are consuming has "dead" calories, is extremely high in sodium or sugar, or is overly processed.

I begin most of my mornings with a nutrient-dense meal because that tactic sets the tone on how I will feel internally with my rationale and how I will effectively perform at my workplace. There simply is no way around it; we must prioritize, and we all must do the work.

Here is something to contemplate as I pose this question. How can you effectively visualize your ideal self if the food you consume is heavily processed and has no nutritional value at all? Junk food puts an extreme setback to the way you think and how your electrical brain signals fire off within you. On the flip side, if you consume nutrient-dense meals/snacks, a different type of energy releases that is so contrary to what you feel when you have the "sugar rush" or the quick "high." If there is one executing tactic that you can do now for yourself, it is to start with one solid healthy meal/snack at a time and just focus on taking it one day at a time.

Through the several years on my first two transformation attempts, I underwent small lessons and adjustments with my food consumption. My first attempt I tried to out-gym nutrition; my second attempt I tried to outrun nutrition. However, my third attempt was most successful because I embraced the idea of making nutrition work for me instead of against me. I interlaced everything together, plus I had mentorship of an amazing community that has also helped me make positive strides toward bettering my health.

# Chapter 2

## *Perception*

*Be thankful for what you have; you'll end up having more. If you concentrate on what you don't have, you will never, ever have enough.*

—*Oprah Winfrey*

Undergoing a health transformation takes everything you have internally and externally. Day in and day out, it is going to coerce you to focus on every decision and test you on every action you take. Not every day is going to be smooth sailing, and there are days where you feel you are on top of the world. I feel it is so important to be mindfully reflective on both good and bad days so you can catch how you are thinking and feeling in those moments. So, this chapter we are discussing perceptions, and I will share with you a moment in my health process that was positively influential toward me.

If there is one golden nugget about the aspect of perception, it's this: It is not about the visuals of how you look and how athletic you are, it is genuinely about the vibes, your intuitions, and the feelings you exude around your environment. Have the sense of urgency on the attitude of appreciating the good traits that you have and exude to others. Put into practice spending a fraction of your day thinking about the great things you possess in your life. This could be anything that ranges from your personal life to professional career.

There needs to be a rewire on your approaches and thoughts regarding what you perceive as normal. If change is to occur, those changes won't happen if you are still practicing the same habitual patterns you have been accustomed to. Those old patterns need to be released, because if you hoard them, the new transition will not occur. It ends up just being thoughts held in stagnation without any means of growth evolving around them. When you build new pathways and patterns in your mind, that is when transformation begins. You will need to negate what you want to execute for your physicality to alter because it starts in the mind.

It will make a world of difference if you can be consistent and take a proactive stance with these strategies. Remember this altering pattern of thoughts: there is a difference between needs, wants, and shoulds. I should be doing this, and I should not be doing that. Well, how far exactly will that take you? There are a lot of people who need to make a shift on their health and wellness. But how badly do they want it? Your shift must come from a "wanting" state of mind, and your "why" must be rooted deep within your mentality to spread toward your soul because this is how you will show up for yourself. I wanted to change because I deserved it, and my "why" is so powerful it drives me to tears to this day.

When I began my transition into this third transformational experience, I already knew that this time around it was going to be different on my end. Take note, my perception going into this third attempt was already on a positive note. I knew I was going to come out truly stepping into my power and dominating the process of becoming healthy. Along the past two decades, I have encountered adjustments and lessons based on health and exercise, and my background as a physical educator assisted me along as well.

Perception is a phenomenal concept. Your mind can think of things that have not come to fruition in reality, yet it can skew your judgment and rhythm toward your intentions. I put emphasis on this notion because it has happened to me numerous times. As people, we have this tendency of perceiving things from the outside in. Let's face it, the wow factor on transformations is when we look at before and after pictures and see how different that person looks. But that's only the tip of the iceberg! People will not know the story behind the glory. The work you put in, the planning, the reflecting, the meditating, they won't see any of that! This is a poignant factor you will need to embrace, acknowledge, and accept.

Motivation and accountability can only go so far, you need to step into the light and discover your power. Let's see it from the other side though; for the most part, a good number of people will notice your transformation even before anything visible happens! They will sense it in your energy and vibe, not to mention your attitude. My outlook changed for the better on the second week of my transformation process. I looked in the mirror and stepped on the bathroom scale, and there was visibly no progress or drop on the scale reading. What was happening is the truest sense and representation on what a health transformation is about. I knew in my heart that I needed to be modest on my approach to the transformation and that my "why" was the driving force so I could be persistent. I was transforming from the inside out.

In general, people think transformations are so farfetched and unattainable because of the time it takes. In a realistic sense, however, transformations are dictated by the way you perceive and internalize. In my case, it took two weeks for people to notice my vibes. Energetically, I felt a big positive difference one month into the process. And to my own surprise, people started to notice a physical difference after only two full months. Slowly but surely, I found myself cleansing my mind and soul, and then the weight loss and improved physique became the byproduct of the process. Modesty over vanity all day, every day, come what may, all the way!

## Modesty Over Vanity

Society tends to look at someone's physique as the transformation "end all," and I am here to state that it is more than just that. For some reason, we tend to get so caught up with numbers. Numbers and percentages are just reference points one can utilize to raise self-awareness.

The vanity I am emphasizing is the showcase of it all. It only portrays the glitz, glamour, and astonishment of someone's physique after the transformation. I am not saying that is a bad thing; all I want to address is that the work and the hardship always has to be done and contended upon. When you hit the gym or running trails, your workouts should not be about how much weight you are lifting or pressing, neither is it about how many miles you are running or pedaling on your bike! Please realize, the outer finished product of your physical appearance is only the beginning of it all. It simply is a checkpoint of the overall journey.

Execution of exercise is not about looking for someone else's validation of approval; this is all about you taking ownership of your control and personal empowerment. This has more to do with your inner relationship with yourself, how you view and treat people, how you perform in your career, and the ability to appreciate/celebrate small victories along the experience. Let us view another perception from the standpoint of Olympic gymnasts and figure skaters. As viewers and sports fans, we only see the finished product of their hard work unfold when they perform their specific routines during Olympic competitions. What we do not ever witness are the athlete's countless hours of practice, athletic training, hardships, breakdowns, breakthroughs, and persistence the previous four years before the event. There is always and forever will be a story behind the glory, and most often, not all days are good days with these athletes trying to fulfill their dream of placing for an Olympic medal, let alone a gold medal.

Having a sense of modesty is key during this process of change. Take in and welcome the compliments others give you, but at the same time, avoid those words from getting way too much into your mind to the point where you get complacent. A little bit of complacency is okay, but too much of it will send you into your comfort zone. I am not perfect in this area myself, and I continue to make positive steps in this matter. Modesty will assist you on internalizing compliments (and remarks) to keep yourself at bay and to keep you focused on your long-range goals. You are the author, coordinator, producer, and director of your story. Your glory will impact others based on how you conduct yourself through your perceptions.

# Chapter 3

## *Preparation and Time Management*

*The key is not the will to win. Everybody has that.*
*It is the will to prepare to win that is important.*

—*Bob Knight*

The obvious given for all of us is we have an allotted twenty-four hours in one day. Time management has been and always will be a constant opponent of mine. I always have to remind myself that time is used in three ways. You are either wasting time, spending time, or investing time. There are other days where I have felt that I did a great job with time utilization, and some where I am guilty of just letting it flow like a river and not doing anything with it. Behind the principle of time management is preparation. Preparation contributes as a monumental factor and touches on all three categories of the mind, spirit, and physical. Whether you are preparing for the daily grind of family life, your profession, coaching a sports team, performing in sports, scheduling, or even a health transformation, there is no doubt in my mind that preparation will take time.

The puzzle piece that joins preparation is prioritization. I view prioritization as a pendulum that swings from one sector to the other, both with extreme measures. You are either prioritizing time to make gains or wallowing it away. With time, there is no constant or manner of neutrality. Moreover, when you first start out with your preparation, it will probably not look, feel, or be ideal to you. However, it is within your persistence and your dedication to improve during these transitional times that's very relevant. Over the course of repetition, you will tend to get more of a fluidity and flow to plugging in what is more meaningful when you prepare. What truly matters are the baby steps of adjustments that you are willing to put forth.

When you hear people bicker about not having enough time, all that equates to is, "that is not on my list of priorities." It is not that they do not have the time for it, it just means that it is not important to them—whatever it is. Until one can observe/feel that disconnect and correlation, that is when the priorities will adjust. For the sake of a wellness transformation, the key to meal prepping is maybe the most important factor in attaining any type of progression. With that mentioned, we all must acknowledge that meal prepping has to be on our top list of priorities.

## Meal Prepping

If there is one thing that I really geek out on, its cooking and culinary arts. I have been cooking for two and a half decades now, getting pointers from my parents, aunt, and then eventually watching celebrity chefs on their how-to programs on television. Meal prepping can feel like an arduous chore for a lot of people, but for me it's one of the most enjoyable parts to a health transformation.

For many, cooking is trivial, but I feel it's a skill everyone must have because it opens a lot of doors and avenues not only from a health aspect but with your precious usage of time. Cooking allows you to build socially with your family and friends. People who appreciate the art and science of cooking have an advantage when going into the process of a health transformation. I will discuss more about food in Part III of this book, but for now, I want to address how I meal prep and the thinking that revolves around it.

Meal prepping can be executed in a variety of ways, but you will have to find the most effective way to do it for yourself and your family. I will not sugarcoat the situation; meal prepping will get tougher on you depending on if you get a professional career change or are married with kids versus if you are living alone and single. If you are persistent enough though, you can easily adjust to those changing factors in your life. With work and my side gig, my schedule will change from week to week.

On my end, I feel that it is important that I stay one to two steps ahead. Here is what I mean by that statement: if my schedule has me off from work on a Tuesday and Thursday on a random week, I am choosing one of those days as a "cook day." Traditionally in most cases/households, Saturdays and Sundays are the days off. The routine will be more set-in stone than my case where I have any random day of the week off from work. In the scenario where if you have a family, this is where the spouse plays a vital role in this process. Remember, it should not feel like a chore; the meal prep activity should be a time where you can bond with your spouse and then eventually when your kids get older, they can have assigned tasks as well. This is all dependent on how you set the environment for yourself and family members. Even when kids are at a young age like four to six, you can give them age-appropriate duties so they can feel involved in the process. Muscle-memory preparation and experiences you build with your kids are memorable for them. In the long run, they may end up appreciating you for the fact that you went over this process with them.

With regard to quantity, you want to prep enough food where if you have a string of days in a row where you are at work, it should fulfill your breakfast, lunch, and dinner. If this is not possible, you want to at least fulfill two out of the three meals per day. There are myriad reasons why you would want to commit to take on this tactic in this manner. On the back end of your work week, you will realize that the meal prepping will not only save you time but money as well.

The meal prep will put you more at ease as you handle your daily duties in your career and family life. The last thing you would want to do is to prepare dinner after a hard day's work. The meal prep will enable you and your family to come home and devote time to different familial needs. With regard to kids, I firmly believe if you catch them at the right age and introduce this tactic as a weekly health routine, it will benefit them in the long run. Communicate to them on the importance of prepping meals from home and let them know why it is important to do this because they have inquisitive minds and will question the intention. Let them know that the assistance they give you in the kitchen is valuable and that you appreciate their contribution. Kids observe and absorb factors to their environment very well, and parents must provide an appropriate setup for them when it comes to prepping meals.

Another characteristic I want to point out: prepped meals will prohibit you from making bad eating decisions when you are on the go. We live in a world now where people want everything fast, convenient, and easy. As a result of that statement, if we choose something that is convenient to eat, there is a high probability that meal you choose to consume will not be nutrient dense in comparison to a prepped meal from home. This is the era I personally coin as the Drive-Thru Generation. With the implementation of Netflix, Amazon, Uber, and GrubHub, we do not even have to travel outside of our homes to get the necessities and conveniences we want.

The sedentary lifestyle in a way is taking over the once active lifestyle this planet had long ago. Therefore, I always preach to my circle of people, "If you sit, you are not getting fit and your health will take a hit." If you contemplate it, this phrase can apply to both exercise and meal prepping. Do you choose the hardship of making a solid effort on making your own food, or will you choose the convenient, easy way out? There is a give and take on both situations—not to mention a big inconvenience. It is a lifelong obstacle to stay, perform, be, and act healthy! It is more difficult to be unhealthy. Life is tough, and it will throw so many twists and turns on us.

My philosophy is, life is difficult as is, but I'd rather deal with the day-to-day grind of life when I am optimized at my healthiest state I can be! This is dependent on my actions in the kitchen when I prep my food and the actions I take while I am exercising in the gym or outdoors.

## Correlations

Time is a precious commodity in our lives. We want to be in a state where we can fulfill and utilize most of the twenty-four hours for meaningful action each day. I will admit a vulnerability that I am struggling with at this moment, because in the past it wasn't an issue with me. I am struggling on waking up a little bit earlier these days, and I will tend to sleep in that extra two hours. Those extra hours can mean the difference in getting productivity into motion and making more use of my time. Here's the correlation I want to place relevance on. Preparation will equate to time usage whether you are exercising, cooking/meal prepping, or scheduling out your calendar.

In whatever profession one is a part of, there is a level of planning that needs to take place. I was a former physical education teacher, and I had days where I did not plan effectively ahead of time, and there were times where I planned accordingly. It made a huge difference when I meticulously planned my lessons appropriately because the activities flowed efficiently, and the kids actively participated because of the clear instructions.

Here's my theoretical question: If we can plan and prepare for the sake of our health and wellness the way we prepare for our careers/jobs, wouldn't that be worth putting forth an honest effort in that sense? We prepare and plan for our jobs, prepare and plan for our households, prepare and plan for other miscellaneous things. But we often forget to plan and prepare for our own health and wellness! Or we do have the intention to focus more on our own health, but too often the idea gets thrown to the backseat of the van. The intentional thought is present, but the execution is not. There has to be a compromising consideration to this matter because all too often we put others first before ourselves!

For the most part, engulfing yourself into this mode of thinking will be challenging. However, there will come a time where you will feel much more at ease with yourself and how you act toward the people in your life. For some, it will take longer than others, but one thing is for sure: the grass is greener on the other side.

# Chapter 4

## *Reception*

*I believe whenever you're trying something new,*
*it's always going to get some kind of bad reception.*

—*Lil Nas X*

Before I get into the content of this chapter, I want to spend time with this great quote. When you encounter and journey into a health transformation, you will need to embrace the simple fact that this is a new lifestyle you are partaking in for the rest of your life. It is not just so you can do for some months and look good for a while and then relapse to your old habits. This endeavor requires you to be the best version of yourself to others in your close circle and the people you will meet in the distant horizon. It is your obligation to be that inspirational figure in their lives.

With that mentioned, it is a guarantee that you will get good and bad reception. When I started my lifestyle results-oriented transformation in the fall of 2018, it felt brand new to me. I was given a blueprint guide that was very simple to follow, and the impression that I got right away was that it seemed very sustainable, which, turns out that it was. However, some of the people in my realm, outside looking in, were saying, "Oh, Brandon is trying to lose weight again, let's see how that's going to turn out." For the most part though, I had a solid support system of encouraging people.

Within those great people supporting me, there are those few who will throw skepticism and shade on you. In reference to Lil Nas X's quote, you can indeed experience bad reception by trying something new! The notion I want to add on top of this quote is sometimes our powerful minds can cause disturbances in the interpretations of that good or bad reception. We have a dynamically unique way of internalizing reception from other people's thoughts and words.

We are our own worst critic where positive and negative self-talk plays such an influence in our lives. I am continuing to be a work in progress when it comes to reception. In the past, whenever I received great compliments from another person, I said to myself, "Oh, they are just trying to be nice to you." I mean, what a terrible way to shut down something that was positive toward me, right? Not to mention, if a negative remark was said to me, I would internalize it and say to myself, "They are probably right." I had to reprogram my way of thinking so I did not fall into negativity. My transformation has taught me to have a more caring heart and outlook on life.

This issue is still and always will be a challenge for me, and I must keep reminding myself that I am good enough and I have what it takes. When verbal compliments come my way these days, I always send a big smile toward them and say, "Thank you, much appreciated."

As mentioned before, there will be tough days and stretches during your wellness journey. Keep in mind that you are the person you spend the most time with. It has been that way since day one, and it will hold true till the day you leave this planet. Be kind and loving toward others, but most importantly, be kind and loving to yourself because that's the best reception you can gain. Not to mention, your number one fan is you.

## Reverting

I had a client that I was mentoring on this new wellness journey, and after a solid forty-fifty days on the lifestyle system, I complimented how well the progression was going. As time went on, however, my client seemed to be unwilling to do the work and started to lose belief. In the end, my client ended up not following through on the journey and simply reverted to that former person in the beginning of it all. It is interesting how people interpret progression and positive words thrown their way. This person ended up ghosting me and my teaching principles. I gave great feedback on the job being done, but it was almost as if the positive reception scared my client, and he ended up afraid of attaining success.

With some people, they enjoy and embrace compliments, and it makes them stronger. In my case, I make sure I acknowledge and celebrate the compliments. Eventually though, I would have to let it go because if I dwell on those confidence-building compliments too much, I get afraid that complacency will settle into my mindset, which will in turn cause me to revert to my old ways. I stated this before, and I will do it again; a health and wellness transformation will take everything you've got and then some! It will test your fortitude and how efficiently well you can eliminate bad habits and formulate good habits.

Part of the mental game is how you react to the reception of other people and at the same time how you yourself internalize those positive and negative words. You will get people who will hate on you. To my surprise, I received that unwanted bad reception from people I did not expect it from. I have friends who went through incredible transformations within the same wellness system, and they got bad reception from the people who were the closest to them. It may happen to you as well. My question to you is, how will you use that so it aids you? Personally, I love getting "hated" on nowadays because it makes me work harder. I can turn their feelings toward me as positive reinforcement to benefit my behalf.

## Nonverbal & Verbal Gestures

Never ever forget the reception you receive from people! The good, bad, beautiful, and ugly can work in your favor in the long run. To this day, I can recall all the fabulous compliments said to me in the past five years I have been on this journey. Here is something to try out with the people who have given you the reception. For the most part, you will have your typical "great job," "you look great," etc. But there are some who will give you different words of adulation, and these are the compliments I urge you not to forget.

As time rolls along, go back to the person who gave you that precious complimentary reception and tell them, "I remember when you told me that . . ." When you do this, it makes the other person feel so good about themself, and then you get to relive the whole reception over at a different joyous level. For some reason, when you recall something emotional (whether it is good or bad), your feelings escalate more when you relive it as opposed to when it first occurred.

I do this all the time with the people who have given me support through my journey. Implement this tactic to rekindle positive feelings and to let others know how appreciative you are of them. This simple act will show your attitude of gratitude to the other party. If they see those actions made by you, it will motivate them to be kind and supportive toward their circle of friends and family. For the people who have given you the skeptical remarks or bad emotional remarks, you don't have to say one word to them. The nonverbal gesture of a great smile or wink of an eye will suffice. You want to embrace only the positive aspects that come from a health transformation. There is absolutely no room for negativity anywhere in this process. Recognize the haters, and if you hear the bad verbal distortion, swipe it away like it was an annoying insect on your shirt, and move on!

# Part I Implementation:

# *Nourishment for Thought*

Everything that encompasses a transformation all comes back to your mentality. You can hit the gym for two hours every day and run miles and miles to get physically fit, but if your mind is not where it's supposed to be, none of that will matter. You can listen to motivational speakers, attend church services, and attend personal development workshops to enrich your soul, but if your mind is not where it's supposed to be, none of that will matter. If your mind and way of thinking is not at your most appropriate state, nothing will function the way you want things to pan out.

Most of the time, people wait around for some external divine force to miraculously save them and pull them out of the debts and abyss of their wellness state. I am writing this book to show readers what is possible. Look at me as your professional tour guide who shows you the doors you can open and the doors you need to be mindful of before you open them. The real heroics will stem from your actions and how you will inspire people in your environment. Grasp hold of your true beliefs, dig down, and gain control!

You will find more material regarding the matter of mindful mentality in my Connect With Me & Free Resources section at the conclusion of this book.

# Part II:
# Spirituality & Emotions

*You can't have a physical transformation until you have a spiritual transformation.*

*—Cory Booker*

# Chapter 5

# *Vindictive Intentions*

*There are only two options regarding commitment. You're either in or out. There's no such thing as a life in between.*

—*Pat Riley*

As mentioned in Chapter 3, preparation is important behind your mindset. Let's dig a little bit deeper and peel another layer behind the idea of preparation. To me, intention is the foundation of any action you partake in, especially when it comes to your health transformation. It is truly the soul backbone and drive behind your journey. Your intentions must be so convincing and specific to whatever goal you are trying to reach that it casts a visualization that is so clear for manifestation to occur.

Take moments during your day to implement and form your intentions. Intentions enable you to stretch your vision, for you to achieve heights you never thought you would reach. Very similar to goal setting, intentions are either on the short term or long term. Contemplating intentions could be done while you are doing meditative exercises, your commute to your workplace, or during a simple walking session around your neighborhood block.

Creating and honoring the commitment to follow through on your intentions is another step in this process that needs careful consideration. Intent from your behalf is the most powerful tool you can possess, and this notion can function not only for health transformations but in any realm of your existing life.

Executing those intentions fuels transcendency that will take you past the expectation you probably anticipate. If you create your intentions the evening before, prior to going to bed at night, verbally say a resounding "Yes" as you wake up the next morning because you will have that opportunity to follow through! Continue to honor your small intentions every day. You will then reach your long-term intentions to fulfill those goals and have resolution present in your life. You get to define your life's purpose and pursue things that bring you an abundance of joy.

Intentions allow you to celebrate wins big and small and let life unfold organically. Moreover, they will enable you to produce wellness contributions around your inner circle that can have meaningful impact of positivity. Nothing was more memorable to me with this occurrence when it happened during my first month of transformation.

## My First Month

The first thirty days of my wellness system was the catapult to how my journey has panned out so far. Two weeks into the lifestyle adjustment, my coworker at the time already noticed something different in me. She mentioned how much more vibrant I was looking after such a short time. She articulated how much more energetic I was looking but really did not comment on weight loss (until much later in the journey).

This occurrence caught me by surprise because it got me thinking how effectively I can work this system at such a rapid manner. My coworker was noticing a change in my attitude, an elevated sense of vivaciousness to my inner spirit. Due to the fact I was intentional with the process, I released visceral fat around my organs that was contributing to the toxicity I had internally. I dropped seventeen pounds and twenty-plus inches around my body in thirty days, but those statistics were not the highlight on that first month. I immediately noticed how my wardrobe was fitting me better and how my body felt lit up with energy.

It was only obvious how good I was feeling because I was fueling my body with the most appropriate nutrition. I started to become a better performer at my workplace. I was outworking my peers who were ten to twenty years younger than me, and because of the dense nutrition I was on, I got stronger as work shifts went on as opposed to the norm where people tire out toward the end of their eight-hour shifts. Slowly but surely, other people were noticing my vibrance and were so impressed by how much progress I made in such a short period.

The lesson I learned in this month was so humbling. It was not about the weight loss, but it was about my spirit being uplifted because of my daily intentions and how my relationship positively changed with nutritional eating and with food overall.

## Surprises

As an elementary school kid, I became enamored with the Lakers/ Celtics rivalry throughout the 1980s. It was maybe one of my fondest memories of my childhood that carried me through my early teens. Years after that decade of basketball showmanship, a few documentaries were made profiling this rivalry that revolutionized not only the game of basketball but made an impact all around the world. I remember watching one piece of a documentary on how Celtics great Larry Bird prepared and diligently worked on his craft. Not only did he make field goals look so easy, but he also made these baskets when his team needed it most during the clutch. Basketball fans watched in awe and amazement as Larry performed and played the game so hard.

A media reporter asked, "Do you surprise yourself sometimes on how you play the game?" Larry Bird's response to this question resonated and has stuck with me to this day. He said, "With the work I put in, there are no surprises. It's expected."[1] Larry hit the nail on the head with this response.

If you put work toward a craft, you can expect the outcomes to be in your favor, no exceptions. When I made humongous strides during my first month and eventual first year of my transformation, I noticed a lot of jaws dropping around my circle. I am not sharing this occurrence to brag about my accomplishments. I am addressing what needs to be present in your inner spiritual core. You may

---

1. Quinn Bucker, *ESPN 30 for 30,* "Celtics/Lakers: Best of Enemies, Part I,", directed by Jim Podhoretz, ESPN Films, episode aired June 13, 2017.

surprise many people with a physical transformation, but if you put in the work, you should expect the outcome you want with no surprises from your end of things.

I must point out though, within this concept lies the double-edge sword. If you embrace the amazement and surprise too much, you can break your fluidity within your work. It will sneak into your mind to the point where complacency can take over. Acknowledge the surprise and kind words from other people, then celebrate those small victories. However, you will need to put those occurrences in the vault, lock it up, and move on with the process.

Your intention is to get to the other side where that grass is greener. Where the grass is greener simply means your optimal manner of living. You can disagree or agree, but your intentions should not be focused on numerical statistics of body fat percentage, number of pounds lost, or how many days in a row you went to the gym. These aspects are a fraction of the transformation process, but it should not be the sole reason of why you undertake this journey! You are prognosticating your mind and soul to the bigger dream life on that side of the spectrum!

Let me be clear with something though, the "greener side" does not mean it will be roses and rainbows all the time. The "greener side" is your genuine ability to function in optimization when challenges come about in your life. Once you arrive at the "greener side," that does not mean you stop! You must continue with purposeful power because this is just the beginning of your new transformed journey.

Life is hard enough as is, you need to be at your healthiest to overcome adversities as opposed to being in a rut and undernourished. The surprise will only last for a short time. What becomes timeless is the constant hunger to inspire others and to lead by example. That attitude is rooted on how powerfully consistent your intentions are.

# Chapter 6

## *The People in Your Life*

*People in your life usually have four purposes. 1)to add 2)subtract 3)multiply or 4)divide. Choose wisely!*

—Jalen Rose

The phrase "it takes a village" holds absolute truth for progression and growth to transpire. The wellness transformation journey may look like its individualized, but there is always a core of people either influencing or detracting from a person. The inner circle of people (which consists of friends, family, colleagues, and mentors) can make or break your psychological way of thinking and reacting. It is so important to surround yourself with people who will praise you with recognition when you have victories.

I am not an expert on matching people and personalities, but you do become the expert on what type of people to surround *yourself* with as time rolls on. You will need people who bring you up when you are not feeling at your best internally. To this day I have a few people in my inner circle who believe in me more than I believe in myself. Hold onto those who build you up, notice your true worth, and have an endless amount of kindness and authenticity. The people in your life are contributing factors to both good and bad memories you attain and the knowledge you want to gain. Memories serve as a contributing reference point for you while you're on a health journey. It is so imperative to use your memories as either a motivation or influencing component. From my end, I experienced frustration and toxicity with those individuals who were negative around my environment. On the flip side, I experienced growth and joy with the people who gave me positivity.

## Frustration and Toxicity

I referenced a quote from Tony Robbins in Chapter 1 regarding focus and energy flow. His quote can hold true to the type of people surrounding you. The toughest experience for me to grasp on to were issues of acceptance, comparisons, and fitting in with the crowd. Being the chubby kid all throughout my childhood, I struggled with this social scenario. To some degree, I think we all struggle with this even now as adults, but in my case, I have attained more effective mindfulness to deal with it. Your energy is a valuable asset to your everyday functioning. That energy can either work to your advantage or disadvantage depending on how you use it.

A vulnerability of mine that I deal with all the time, is that my emotions are my greatest strength and weakness. I have come across some painfully hard lessons on how to harness my frustrations, and over the years, I am gradually getting better. Personally, I do not deal well with people who like to gossip, excessively complain, and give off negative vibes. I refute to affiliate with people of this manner because that depletes me.

I will delve into the aspect of frustration on Part III: Physical later in the book, but frustration in this sense (in the emotional side) is a different feeling. What builds upon the frustration when other individuals are involved is the feelings of confrontation and questioning if you are good enough to be accepted. Combine all those negative aspects together; that is when the toxicity occurs. Toxicity can lead to many different unwanted avenues because if you are toxic in your soul, there is a carryover effect that may skew your physical/mental well-being and not to mention how you perceive things. As young teens transitioning to young adults, we all go through this stage in our lives, and we all handle these situations to the best of our ability. But if we have a strong support system of people to mentor and guide us from the very start, it's more manageable to deal with this life obstacle.

My issue with frustration and toxicity stemmed back a few years ago when I was a candidate for a promotion at my job. Out of all the candidates that were up for the two available spots, I knew in my heart of hearts I would be able to land one of those two slots. When my boss called me into the office and notified me that I did not get the position, I was livid. Initially, I reacted this way because of the other workers that were with me as candidates. Let's just say, I was the more efficient and harder worker among all of them.

Sometimes the ball does not bounce in your favor. The company was looking for someone else with another personality to best suit the job description. The two people who attained the promotion were close friends of those supervisors who evaluated the process. A part of me thought it had nothing to do with the quality of worker I was but the type of people in that higher power at my job. At the time it happened, I carried a grudge. My composure and poise became nonexistent, and I boiled over in emotion.

I mentioned before how my emotions are my greatest strength and weakness, and clearly in this scenario, it proved to be my weakness. As a matter of fact, as I am writing this, I am experiencing all those feelings of uneasiness and frustration as I recall this life event of mine that happened nearly five years ago. This is the power of your personal memories. I must be cautious on how I utilize memories because if it's a negative memory, most likely I will be much angrier when I reminisce about it versus how mad I was at the time it happened. Days after that reveal, my coworkers sensed concern over me because I was disgusted about the promotion, and I got called in to consult with my team leaders. They inquired if everything was okay, and I held a poker face and told them everything was fine. Then my boss shared with me that I was called in here because "the team members were worried about how you were acting."

Looking back at it now, there was a part of me that wished I could have expressed my true feelings in that moment, but I was afraid to cause more tension around the workplace. The one real disturbing occurrence was how it was eating away at my soul, and I did not have the fortitude to let it go after several days. Within a week after that office consultation, I got my mind to straighten out so I could think more rationally, and I ended up causing a change within my work environment that I did not anticipate.

## Growth and Joy

The silver lining in this experience was that every day since that evaluation period, I made it a point to not only outwork the two people who got the promotion, but I wanted to outwork every team member in the company. I was months into my transformation lifestyle, and I had the supplemental nourishing fuel to back up my performance. I intently raised my level of exuberance with customer service and displayed an upbeat energy with my work ethic. I constantly oozed positivity and confidence. I wanted to do this for myself *and* prove to the company that I was one of their best.

Did it make much of an impact with my supervisory team, probably not. To be quite honest, I found some of the supervisory team to be toxic in spirit, and those few people probably did not gravitate toward me because of how I was working. These individuals did just enough to attain that higher power so that they can have comfort on their day-to-day. I wanted to cause positive impact for the people who noticed my worth in the work environment, and not to mention the customers who came into the store consistently. As a matter of fact, I received much praise and appreciation, more from customers than I did with my own coworkers.

I found growth in detracting myself from those negative people and giving my full attention to the ones who valued my worth. All the kind words they poured into me, I returned with much gratitude toward them. My heart and soul were full! I found so much more peace with myself, and not to mention, I became one of the best performers at the job, all thanks to the way I conducted my health and wellness. At this junction of my job, I mainly focused and poured love to the coworkers and customers who constantly gave me praise. I sensed uneasiness from the people who could not or refused to jive with my high vibes. I did not care if they spoke negatively behind my back, I did not care how I was portrayed because I was in control of my spiritual emotions.

What I have slowly learned over time is that I will not make everyone happy. Being selective on who gets and receives your energy is self-care. There is no greater gift than realizing that you are of high worthiness and that your personality is enough.

## Why This Matters

I recalled this life experience of a missed job promotion because it was not a lesson of how I performed and behaved at my workplace. The lesson I gained was the ability to reflect on how I handled my emotions. The relevance within this was to put on display one of my biggest weaknesses and show my vulnerability. In retrospect, I have gotten just a little bit better at acknowledging my emotions when things do not sway in my favor. I have learned to remove myself from the situation and see things from the outside as if I were evaluating and eventually communicating to myself spiritually.

Have I lost my composure and poise since this work incident? Yes, of course! I am only human, and we as a species can only take so much before we lose our sense of calm. This life event had nothing to do with my health transformation but, in a way, has a lot of intertwining characteristics. If you are rattled and angry at any workplace environment, there is no way you are going to function well. The same exact thing can be said while undergoing a health transformation! Emotions must be at the most appropriate place in your soul to perform effectively with excellence.

# Chapter 7

## *Every Body Is Different*

*Too fat, too skinny, too short, too tall, too anything! There's a sense we're all too something, and we're all not enough. This is life. Our bodies change, our minds change, our hearts change.*

—*Emma Stone*

The comparison game is the ultimate one-way ticket to discouragement! This game is where you catch yourself going around in circles with no end point and finding no solution to your journey. I use the powerful word of *shame* here in a sense that it will deflate your innermost morale during a transformation. "She is so much prettier than her," and "He is so much cooler than me!" Comparison is the dream-killer when it comes to your pursuit of health optimization.

I am not going to claim that I have never compared myself to others in the past. I too have gotten caught in this spider web, but it's up to you to decide how you internalize it you and move on. The purpose of this chapter is to give insight, raise awareness, and give consideration. I am not a scientist, nutritionist, or personal trainer who will discuss fat percentages, body types, muscle-to-fat ratio, or bone density.

We are all from different walks of life, different regions all over the world, different set of genetics from the generations that came before us, different cultures, and with different upbringings and sets of beliefs. Avoid making comparisons of how you look and how you function versus others. Everyone is their own unique individual with their own skill sets, talents, mentality, and gifts.

Avoid comparing your progress with another person who is also going through a health/weight loss transformation. Your page nine is not the same as someone else's chapter five of their progress. Celebrate the fact that you are making progress and are feeling better about yourself. The only person you should be competing against and comparing yourself to is you. You are in competition with yourself from yesterday, last week, last month, and so on. You are striving to be better than you were as each day passes along.

## Celebrities, Athletes, and Us

We tend to observe and compare ourselves to the individuals with higher stature, fame, wealth, and popularity. Celebrities and athletes hold a sense of power when it comes to appearance and living a lavish life. I remember back in my teen years how all the girls would look at pop culture magazines and wish they were as pretty as this actress or model or look as good as this other celebrity and what not. The boys would wish they were as cool and as athletic as Michael Jordan or their preferred sports star.

I remember Michael Jordan and Charles Barkley were featured in McDonalds and Snickers Commercials. I said to myself, "Well, if

Jordan and Barkley are consuming McDonalds and Snickers candy bars, then I will too!" I wanted to be athletic like they are so why not, right? I was a young kid, what did I know about the psychological power behind television commercials? What tasted so deliciously sweet and savory was really a detriment to my health. I did not know that those were advertisements geared to make money, thus having total disregard to human health/wellness.

Reflecting on this, I realize how much an effect advertisement can have on people. Another element we all need to remember is that celebrities have high incomes that can support whatever fitness goals they have, whereas the average person needs to divert to different options because the income is not the same.

I wanted to address this experience to simply bring attention to the matter of how advertisements have a powerful influence on our brains, especially when our sports heroes or beloved celebrity figures are featured in them. With technology evolving, who knows how much more influential this issue can be. You must take a proactive stance to ward off these revolving variables that go against the principles of a transformation. A lot of this stuff is distortion and white noise that encompass your goals and intentions.

## Patience

My pet peeve when consulting with prospects on changing their health is that they want the transformation right away. Not only will a transformation require everything you got effort wise, but it's also going to test your truest valor of patience. This is not a DoorDash,

Amazon Prime service where these amazing occurrences happen overnight!

Your progress will differ from person to person. The patience and having the acknowledgment on that idea is your key to success. In my case, I made humongous strides on my first two to three months. I may be wrong on saying this, but looking back at that time, I impressed a lot of people with my progress, but at the same time, I felt them thinking, "I am not built the way Brandon is. He lost all that weight in a short period of time."

My colleagues were astonished and confused at the same time. I made observations on the body language on my potential prospects when I conversed with them about the journey, and I could sense their intimidation because of my rate of progression. This is where other people need to realize that every path is different.

The reason why I made early strides is because I was "battle tested" prior to starting my lifestyle program. I made meaningful adjustments with my eating habits that took several years to get accustomed to. So, when I started the lifestyle program, I was already acclimated to the adjusted nutritional habits. My prospects did not know that portion of my experience, they only saw what was on the superficial level—the tip of the iceberg. Many that start this go in without the arsenal that I possessed, not to mention the educational experience I had with human movement.

A racing horse will put on the blinders so they can only see what is in front while they are running that race and not be distracted by what is going on everywhere else. The idea is the same with a health and wellness transformation. Stay the course. The only competition is you, have the patience with your work, and give yourself grace to celebrate your victories. Instead of making comparisons with others, try to draw inspiration from other people who are in that same wellness space with you that will reciprocate support in return and find those similarities so you can enjoy the growth that comes with it.

## Weight Loss versus Weight Gain

If you ponder deeply, what is the first thing that comes into people's minds when they hear the terms *weight loss* and *weight gain*? We can have different interpretations because when you think of *loss,* it is often viewed as negative, and in contrast, gains are interpreted as positive.

At the end of this chapter are two progression pictures of me during my transformational journey. After I accomplished a tremendous weight loss, I went through a period of weight gain. Often, when people go through weight gain, their spirits get demoralized. I inserted this portion of my health transformation in hopes of bringing to light that weight loss and weight gain are not all what they seem to be.

On the left picture I was at 199 pounds, and on the right picture I was at 221 pounds, a gain of twenty-two pounds total. Take notice though, I am wearing the same outfit in both pictures, and the time differential in between each picture was just under eight months. What gets dismissed is that weight gain can be viewed upon as regression or a major setback. These progression pictures are proof that the number on the scale only tells a fraction of everybody's health journey. This portion of my transformation truly defines the title of this book, *Formulation You*!

Lifestyles created with good intentions, rooted with healthy habits, love, and a solid nutritional eating regimen supersede the numerical statistics every time. In the beginning, it is about you and your actions on reaching that ideal self in mind, body, and spirit. Over time, however, it no longer is about you but the person you have become that is making a positive influential impact on others. This is what formulation in the health and wellness space is about! If I consult and coach potential prospects, it is never about me! It is all about my client stepping into and discovering their ideal self; it is about finding a brand-new healthy attitude.

# Chapter 8

## *Older! Not Old*

*Age, what is it? It's not a figure that has ever meant anything to me.*
*—Steffi Graf*

A few years ago, I overheard a fellow coworker talking to others at work one day, and she was alluding to how low her energy levels were and how age was getting to be a nuisance. She went on and claimed, "I just wish I had the energy of a young eighteen-year-old woman." Another coworker said, "I am at age twenty-seven, and I am feeling it already."

My question is, what exactly was "it" that she was feeling? If anything, age twenty-seven is in your peak years. Was she referring to deterioration, because that was the interpretation I got from that eavesdrop. I observed these two coworkers over time and noticed how they were consuming overly processed foods during their breaks and meal periods. On top of that, I constantly saw them sipping on sugary drinks throughout the day. It is no wonder that their energy levels were sapped to nothing with barely any performance output to show for it.

Did I not talk about nourishment earlier in this book? On how it can have both good and bad effects on a transformation? Steffi Graf was one of my heroes growing up. I admired how she always had a solid frame of mind and had mental toughness in her when she competed in the game of tennis. She is older in age now, approaching her mid-fifties, but from the outside, she still looks the same as she did during her playing days. I love her quote about age because it really is just a numerical figure.

I stand by the idea that one's state of mind dictates the true age of a person. Quite simply, if you are thinking that you feel old and run down, that is exactly how you are going to feel. If you attain a positive, high energy and lust for life, then your outlook and impression is one of a person who is young at heart. It does not matter how old you are because anyone can execute this way of thinking.

On this note, didn't I address the notion of energy flow and focus earlier in this book? I purposefully practice mobility exercises, attaining enough sunlight exposure, and drinking enough water to stay youthful in mind and body. When I was a kid, I often heard from elders, "Enjoy being young now, because wait until you get older, your attitude, outlook, and energy will change." More along those lines, I had elder relatives of mine who told me and led off with the phrase, "When you get older, then [this] will occur." In my mind I said to myself, "So what if I get older?" Moreover, I was in total disagreement with their statement about attitude changing as you age! You are in control of your attitude and outlook at all times, and getting older has nothing to do with it.

In my youth deep down, I felt something was off. It was almost as if I was defying what was being told to me. At that age though, I could not articulate what I wanted to express. Looking back at this, I get upset on how my own inner circle fed me these words that led to an incorrect mentality that goes against living a life full of abundance, promise, and vibrance. And then I gave it more thought and reflection.

My relatives back then probably did not know any better and just regurgitated what was taught to them by their elders. I was heading down that same exact road of limiting beliefs until I forged my own way and took ownership of the way I wanted to feel for myself. I wanted more for myself, and the only person I knew who could attain those healthy ways was me, and only me! The desire to make an impactful, beneficial change for myself was my best decision ever.

## Quality

If you are not familiar with the lifestyle of an educator, a lot of work goes in by the teachers after school is dismissed. They can be on campus anywhere from two to four hours after the bell rings and have to repeat that grind over again the next day.

One day during my years in education and athletics, I was speaking with a colleague during our lunch hour, and we were conversing along the lines of quality of sleep and rest. As teachers, having rest is golden to the daily duties we have. We spoke about tactics and supplements to take to ensure quality of sleep. The conversation then went on a tangent regarding age and getting older. I inquired to my colleague, "How much sleep do you get a night?"

She answered me with a resounding "Not much at all." She went on and said, "In fact, Brandon, as you get older the quality of your sleep diminishes significantly, and there is no way around it. The only sleep I really get is when I crash on my recliner with a glass of wine."

On the outside, I acknowledged what she had to say and went along agreeing with her casually, but internally, I was in total disagreement with her. At the time, I did not know how I was going to do it, but I knew as I got older, I would prioritize the quality of sleep and make that health characteristic an important one. Anyone can attain great quality of sleep no matter how old the person is.

Please allow me to be clear: losing quality of sleep because of older age is a complete myth! It is nothing but a false narrative that has been engraved into many minds to think in that manner. Everything circles back to how you are showing up for yourself and how you are treating/nourishing yourself at a consistent basis. There is definitely a proactive way around it, you just have to make the adaptations to acquiring those qualities of rest. I will delve more into this in Part III of this book.

## Alteration

From what I have heard and experienced so far with the people I have come across in my life, we need to make a serious shift on how we view and approach aging. There is this sense of elimination when we ponder how we should be feeling at certain ages. It disturbs me when people are stuck in this mindset of "Enjoy your twenties and thirties because once you hit your forties, it's a completely different set of circumstances."

We need to seriously stop attaching numbers to ourselves on how we should or could be feeling! Moreover, these are the stories that get engraved into the core of your mind when you keep telling yourself it over and over. Imagine mentioning a statement like that to someone in their eighties and nineties! What would their reaction be if they heard that statement about the twenties, thirties, and forties talk? The power to feel so good relies heavily on your soul and state of mind.

Let me put it this way: you do not know how great you can feel until you feel so great! You have the ability and fortitude to feel fantastic all throughout your whole livelihood if you create healthy, consistent habits that support your lifestyle. On my end, I have more energy as a gentleman entering his late forties than when I was in my twenties.

Whenever I hear someone say to me, "I am getting old," I always respond with a stern voice, "No, you are getting older." The term *old* to me is your body in a decrepit state! Old to me is someone lying on their death bed clinging onto their last moments. I seriously feel rewording to "I am getting older" will mean the difference of five to fifteen quality years of your life. This simple switch of your mentality will generate leaps and bounds in formulating a better quality of life because it's a foundational narrative that will implement into your soul.

Think about it, there is a derogative aura when we use the phrase "getting old." "Getting older," to me, sounds more uplifting! The usage of "getting older" sounds more like the individual is gaining more wisdom and progressing into transcendence and evolving at the same time. "Getting old" or "I am old" has this connotation of being done with living. To me that sounds so morbid, and it has this feeling of giving up, giving way, and quitting. Bearing uncontrollable circumstances and God willing, having the experience to beautifully age through the years and decades is a splendid blessing.

There is a fighting champion's heart in all of us to dig deep so we can confront our ideal quality of life on that other side. Finding that champion's heart is dependent on you, your actions, the people you build relations with, and how you rewire your thinking. I will reiterate again: align yourself with like-minded people who share that same toughness as you so you can build each other up. Fears, problems, and obstacles are temporary; your dream life is forever. Believe in the confidence, your clear vision, and your everlasting faith to grow older!

# Part II Implementation:

## *Satiety for the Soul*

Throughout Part II of this book, we touched upon the differentiation of body types, how to approach aging so that your soul can stay youthful, and how the people in your life are dependent of how you progress in your transformation. The other emphasis I want to bring attention to is your surrounding environment. This is yet another important constituent that plays a role in your lifestyle adjustment. This is an underrated factor that intertwines with your emotions and soul.

In a rural area, you have easy access to the outdoors/wilderness versus an urban area where it can be challenging to find parks that can change your views on taking a proactive stance with exercise and activity.

Here are some other questions to consider: What if you are in a certain spot of the nation where farmers' markets and grocery chains are not as present or attainable? What happens then with how you go about the idea of nourishment? As many may already know, these regions in our country are coined as "food deserts." Where food deserts are present, most likely the populous around that area is not getting or receiving proper overall nutrition.

Another alarming factor to be on notice with is a lot of cheap, affordable food is highly processed, high in sugar/sodium, and has dead calories. So, what if you are in an environment where fast food chains are in abundance around your neighborhood? You have the intentions and awareness to change, but how will you maneuver around that overwhelming presence to control your personal health?

How safe is the neighborhood you are residing in? Are the dynamics of the environment safe and conducive enough where you can execute a running or walking schedule, or is the neighborhood unsafe? Unsafe can pertain to common crime around the neighborhood or it can pertain to the dynamics of having simple well-kept sidewalks and traffic signs and lights. I encourage you to be mindful of these variables when you undertake a health transformation. It will mean the difference between you making effective strides on your journey.

# Part III:
# Physical

*The pain that you are willing to endure is measured by how bad you want it!*

—*David Goggins*

# Chapter 9

## *Activity versus Exercise*

*Lack of activity destroys the good condition of every human being.*
—*Plato*

I had a stirring conversation one day with my entrepreneurial mentor, and she mentioned to me that there is "no glory on burning the midnight oil" when it comes to your profession or exercise/fitness. She went on to explain the basis around that quote, and her whole point was to work smarter and more efficiently as you progress as opposed to expending unnecessary energy to fulfill someone else's dream in a professional career and to avoid burnout/injury in physical fitness. I wish I had this conversation in my early twenties because it would have made a difference on how I approached fitness.

For nearly two decades, I was "burning the midnight oil" when it came to fitness and exercise. I carried this mantra of a "no pain, no gain." It was to the point where if I was not profusely sweating, I would translate that workout session as a waste of time because there was no burn. When I went into the gym, I would spend two to three hours per workout session. When I was into distance running, I would do multiple ten-mile running sessions. Nowadays, I think and feel the complete opposite about exercise and activity. I am not saying that I am sedentary, but more of a sense of condensing the sessions that are more physically manageable and not as time consuming.

In this chapter, I will delve into my own thoughts about exercise and activity to discuss the difference between the two characteristics. My goal is to explain the relevance of human movement at its simplest form so that you can develop a course of action (or fitness regimen) that will best suit your goals and endeavors.

## Activity

Activity covers a broad spectrum of movements, and in my honest opinion, everyone (no matter what physical level you are in) needs daily movement. One may ask how much movement is sufficient per day? This is all dependent on how one feels and how efficient they fuel themselves with food and hydration. Generally speaking, thirty minutes of physical activity is needed per day, every day, for the rest of your life! Thirty minutes is a fraction of your day, and I truly believe anyone can allot that time of their twenty-four hours to physical activity.

Activity can range from house chores to gardening to washing the car, and it can be as simple as doing a stroll around the neighborhood block. There is no reason why you cannot implement one to two walking activities per day every day three hundred sixty-five days a year. Barring any physical disabilities or health restrictions, this tactic must be executed and is a nonnegotiable! There is no way around it, and there are no shortcuts.

Heck, if walking around your neighborhood is too boring, do some flexibility/mobility exercises in your living room. On few occasions I will head down to my local driving range and hit a small bucket of golf balls just to clear my mind and get my required thirty minutes of activity. You can even tune into your favorite music playlist and just dance in place for a small period.

Options for activity are limitless, and I will reiterate this notion time and time again throughout the remainder of this book: you need to find movements and activities that you enjoy doing. Moreover, if you can find someone in your family or inner circle of friends that likes the same movements as you, form a tandem with them. The more people you have in your corner, the better the experience is going to be.

One of the most inspirational men I've ever become affiliated with was Monsignor Richard Murray in the parish school I used to work at. Into his early nineties, I saw him moving every day to the best of his abilities, putting in his steps and walking, climbing stairs around the school grounds. His intent was to utilize and maximize his functioning mind and body to the best he possibly could. He always preached to the faculty and students at the school, "If you don't use it, you're going to lose it."

His drive to make the best of what he had during all facets of his life is a true testament on what it means to be active in body, mind, and spirit. I admired what he stood for and followed through on the facets that worked for him best. His impact as a genuine gentleman spoke volumes not only to me but to the other community members of the parish and school.

The reason I referenced Monsignor Murray is because activity will always trounce exercise. What I mean by that statement is I view activity as something that will always be everlasting because anyone (no matter how old or how young) can execute this. Monsignor told me that there was a point in time where he had to stop exercising with fierce intensity because of how much older he was getting. But he still found his own niche to stay active, to stay timeless as long as possible, and what I admired is that he did not use his age as an excuse or a setback.

On a side note, one of the coolest things about him was that he drove a green Ford Mustang and about three years into my tenure at the school, I later found out he had to stop driving because of his age. He did that out of safety because even though he still had his reflexes, him getting older diminished the reaction time needed for driving. He was living at his most optimal level until old age finally caught up to him a few months after he turned 101 years old. The longevity he had was impressive because he was optimally functioning for the majority part of his life.

I mentioned in the previous chapter that aging is a splendid blessing because not everyone in this world gets a chance to experience it. The smaller blessings within his lifetime are the adaptations he got to experience and put on display for others to take notice of. On a side note, he got the tremendous opportunity to witness his own environment grow and develop from the ground up. When the parish school broke ground in the 1960s, he mentioned how vast and open the land was during those days and how there was little civilization.

I look forward to the day in the distant future where I need to make that decision and say, "I am older now, so I will need someone to drive a car for me because my reaction time is not how it used to be." Indeed, that is a phenomenon to be appreciative about because I would be making that adjustment while my brain is fully functioning at an older age. Monsignor Murray, a man full of passionate enthusiasm, ended up passing at 103 years of age.

## Exercise

Compared to activity, exercise is a concentrated practice with a more sustained intensity throughout its sessions. Unlike physical activity, exercise is more strenuous in nature. In my most honest humble opinion, workouts should last no more than sixty minutes unless one is training for some active event. My workouts are about forty-five minutes give or take, and by the end of these sessions, I am totally gassed. Let's reiterate this notion of human movement: activity is to be done every day; exercise is to be performed three to five times a week. Some may disagree with this, and that is fine.

With exercise, my intention is to give focus to a specific fitness component and really involve the brain's activity to correlate with the muscles being trained. In other words, it is as if I am connecting my brain to stimulate muscle activity, which is dependent on what type of exercise I am executing. For example, if I am doing spider crawls, I want to make sure I engage the muscles I am working with each contralateral movement I make with my arm and leg moving forward. I purposefully pause for two seconds after each rep to make sure my breathing is rhythmic and that I am concentrating on the muscles being worked with that particular workout. Cognitively, I want to also make sure I am executing the correct form and technique to that exercise.

In addition, over the course of time I have discovered to really slow down my movements in weight resistance training. Whether using free weights, hex bars, or cabled weights, I deliberately slow down the motions when I reset to a new exercise repetition. This forces your brain to really connect with the muscles being worked on that exercise, and I urge everyone to give this tactic a try. It has opened my horizons on how to train at a more calm, relaxed state. I have learned very slowly over the years that lifting heavy weight is not always the most effective strategy. The quality of movement for me is more relevant than the quantity of the weight. This is a principle I have learned to embrace.

As I mentioned before, I used to partake in half marathon races in my mid- to late thirties. Before, I ran for the sake of training and keeping my cardiorespiratory fitness in check so I could prolong and sustain my sessions. Nowadays, I run to calm my nerves and gain mental clarity before I go in for a work shift or after I finish a work shift. I used to "burn the midnight oil" with my exercise regimen. I am a lover of food so my mentality was to work out as hard as I could so I could consume the food I love. That is obviously the incorrect approach to a healthy lifestyle.

I am a true believer of health being eighty percent nutrition and twenty percent exercise. Now that I fuel myself appropriately, effectively, and properly, my mentality on exercise has shifted. I exercise now to release tension, to celebrate my athletic abilities, alleviate stress, and for the gratitude I have with the usage of my body. Exercise no longer feels like a chore to me, and there is no longer that sensation where it feels like this must be obligatory, nor do I view exercise as a form of punishment because I indulged on palatable foods.

## The Basics

I used to be the person that went to the gym approximately four times a week and relied heavily on the usage of weight machines and free weights. It was conveniently located in my university, and I formed my course schedule around gym time. However, I was not going to be a college student forever, and throughout the years, I had to adjust. These days, I gauge myself on what I call the bare basics of fitness. I gravitated toward this tactic nearly five years ago to make things much easier on me and less time consuming. With all the knowledge of different physical movements I have been exposed to during my education program as a PE teacher, I can easily make routines off the top of my head to the point where exercise comes as second nature to me.

You can effectively get a good exercise session without the use of gym equipment and implement your own body weight as resistance. I mainly give attention to varietal exercises:

- pushups
- crunches/sit-ups

- lunges
- squats
- jumping jacks

I have at least three different renditions to each exercise listed on the bullet points above. I execute this along with the accompaniment of interval running and walking to a point where I can easily be occupying a thirty-to-forty-five-minute time span. This adjustment was practical for me, and I did not have to commute to a gym. I could literally get dressed within a few minutes and just workout on the driveway of my home. You can do what I did as well, but to remind you again, you will decide on what feels best for you. This is all about your transformation and your regimen because you are the one who will put the work in and spearhead the process. Below my advisory note, you can find two sample circuit exercise sessions to experiment the "basics" in action.

***Advisory Note:*** If starting out brand new, I would advise not to do all exercises during a circuit session only because I want to avoid the feeling of overwhelm and intimidation. I started out with three exercises and lowered the repetitions so that each circuit was a manageable ten to fifteen minutes in duration. As time rolls along and consistency starts to creep in, you can increase the number of sets and repetitions as well as your intensity at your own discretion. I am only showing you two sample sessions below, but there are multiple combinations of this circuit once you start exploring more of the movements and discovering how your body feels.

**Circuit #1** (executing the basics as its traditional form of movement)

Sets: 3

Repetitions: 12 times on each exercise

2-minute walk interval in between each set

- Pushups
- Abdominal crunches
- Lunges
- Squats
- Jumping jacks

**Circuit #2** (variable rendition movements of each exercise)

Sets: 4

Repetitions: 8 times on each exercise

3-minute jog/run in between each set

- Spider pushups
- Bicycle crunches
- Curtsy lunge (side to side)
- Air squats (pause for 2 seconds at the bottom)
- Paper doll jumping jacks (arm circles backward)

## An Athlete in All

It is my firm belief that there is an athlete in all of us. I believe we are all talented in some form of movement. Some of us are more rhythmic in movement, and some are just more in tune with athleticism and can fine tune to a sport. Our bodies are meant to move and be active; it has been designed that way for as long as we can date back to our own evolution.

As mentioned in the beginning of the book, I found out about this athletic enlightenment through my training regimen in high school football. This was where everything began for me with my exercise journey. I was automatically placed with a group of guys all geared toward the same goal on prepping their bodies in the spring and summer seasons to get ready for the fall when football came around. It was the first time where exercise and conditioning really entered the core thoughts of my mind, and it gave me the opportunity to launch into a realm I was not familiar with at the time.

For the most part of growing up, I was entrenched in casual movement revolving around recreational play in elementary and middle school. As I got into high school, it was a level up. My coaches developed a routine program on what body foundations to work on as we progressed through our training, and it gave me a glimpse into what it means to prepare for something. I was grateful for the experience I had with high school football because of the camaraderie I built with my teammates, but looking back at it after ten years, even twenty years down the line, this was my foundation of what it takes to move up from an athletic standpoint. The experience was a propeller to the world of exercise. Football taught me the principles of intensity and frequency, which is the segue topic to the next chapter of the book.

# Chapter 10

## *Intensity and Frequency*

*Hard work guarantees you nothing, but without it you don't stand a chance.*
—*Pat Riley*

Intensity and frequency are the cogs to exercise. Nobody in this life of yours is responsible for meeting these two aspects other than yourself. This is why I always tell people I advise, "The workout session you put in is *all you.*" Whenever you hit the gym, run the track, or hike in the wilderness, you are the one who stepped into that occasion to better yourself physically. Before starting a workout, be proud of that accomplishing moment because no one can take that away from you. Take joy and realize you just decided to grasp hold of an opportunity to honor your personal wellness.

Intensity is defined by how hard you are exerting yourself during these exercise sessions. For change in your physical features to occur, you will need to step up your intensity at some point on your wellness transformation. However, I must mention, there is a fine line before you're overexerting yourself, and I will elaborate more on that on the latter chapters of the book.

I translate frequency to how often I am creating exercise opportunities for myself. Frequency stems back to being intentional. It has more to do with your mind and soul than a physical trait. Whether I do a quick twenty minutes or a prolonged workout close to one hour, I am confronted with how hard I am performing and how often I make these sessions available for myself.

## Familiarization

Intensity is a very tricky aspect when it comes to coordinating a workout regimen. Our natural instinct is to go out, get active, and push as hard as we can. You will be setting yourself up for failure either quitting on your health journey or getting physically injured because your mind and body was not ready for that enhanced intensity. All too often, I have witnessed people trying to do too much too soon.

I recently watched the movie *AIR* starring Matt Damon, and in the movie, his character mentioned how he disliked running. At the end of the movie, he decided to hit the track and give running a try, and barely into his first lap of running, he stopped and quit. We all start at letter A, but we want to get to X, Y, and Z over the course of a couple of days. No! We need to stop this type of self-sabotage because it will get us nowhere! Start at A, then slowly work on B and C.

This is all about learning and discovering yourself as an athlete. Familiarize yourself with various types of exercises and gradually go through those movements. Your own body will tell you if you enjoy the challenge or not. The more movements you break down to their fundamental core, the more you can apply them properly to your life. It is almost as if you are in the mode of rehabilitation when you first explore and discover the movements. Attempt the exercises as though you have arthritis in your body so that you execute the exercises slowly. Familiarize before you turn it up!

## Frequency = Consistency

When you practice the art of creating and setting aside time for yourself to exercise, it is obvious you are enhancing the frequency of how often you exercise. Consistency naturally comes into play, and now you have fulfilled this other key component to your wellness journey. How consistent are you with your workout sessions? One of my other vulnerabilities when it comes to consistency is some days, I do struggle finding the will to muster up a sixty-minute workout. In addition to that, are you forming the appropriate habits and behaviors involved when it comes to consistency and frequency?

Ten-to-fifteen-minute exercise increments can go a long way and speaks volumes on positive habit forming, and one may think that the duration may not be effective enough, but I challenge naysayers to view it on another scope. A quick few minutes of light activity is better than doing zero at all. When I mentioned my football training in high school, it was easy for me to execute those workouts because it was already embedded in my daily class schedule. I did not have to think it out because every day I knew from 11:00 a.m. to 12:30 p.m., I was working out and getting stronger day by day. But, as I moved on from high school, that time block for my training was over. As I got into college, and then into adulthood, I always had to search for time to put in frequent workouts throughout the weeks.

You can coerce yourself to have solid frequency, but to be consistent, you will need a firm mindset. Your career, educational endeavors, possibly your marital status, and the decision to have a family will affect your schedule. Changes will occur not only externally but internally as well when you get older. It will challenge you on how well you make positive adaptations. Through it all, consistency and frequency have to be managed and sustained in order to have a shot of attaining that optimal quality of life. Remember this, nobody can take away the hard work you put forth toward exercise, nutrition, and spiritual well-being. The intensity behind your work ethic is rooted within your mind and spirit, and there will be people who may judge you. However, if you know that the intentions stemming from that hard work will benefit you and your family, it does not matter what other people negatively think about you. Sometimes, the people who throw skepticism on your hard work want that for themselves but don't know how to go about achieving it. Hence, reception and perception.

People who do more than you are not the ones who will talk down upon you. It's the individuals who do less than you who will be condescending toward you. Be meticulous, and at the same time, articulate about putting your work ethic on display. Actions truly speak louder than words, and the people who notice are the ones that genuinely matter. The bottom line is what really matters to you and how hard and frequently you are going to work for that ideal vision to manifest itself.

# Chapter 11

# *FOOD: Fuel Not Gas*

*The food you eat can be either the safest and most powerful form of medicine or the slowest form of poison.*

—*Ann Wigmore*

I love food! Food is influential. It brings people together, and it truly is the binder that brings us life. However, I must address that when food rears its ugly head, it can bring the slowest form of painful deterioration. I have experienced both sides, and I am very grateful that I am on the better side of things. The toughest part of the health journey is discovering the pattern and combination of food working to fuel your body as opposed to your body having to work its tail off to break down food. I have a motto I hold closely to heart when it comes to nutrition, and it is, "More commands and less demands."

When you have nutrient-dense foods, it's easier to make commands on how you want your body to perform and function. Those nutrients and vitamins immediately get absorbed by the vital organs of your body to properly serve the purpose of functioning. Foods that are processed and have dead calories will force your body on strenuous demand to metabolize and sort out. This is why you tend to get that sleepy feeling after a heavy meal. All that blood goes toward the process of digestion and results in lethargy.

During my collegiate days, I attended a major league baseball game with my family one evening. What felt like normal eating to me was anything but according to my cousin. She had noticed how much processed food I was consuming that night. Pre-game, we went to a burger joint nearby where not only did I finish my portion of the meal, I consumed others' food that they no longer wanted. I was in the mindset of "I do not want food to go to waste," so I finished up their meals. Then when we arrived at the stadium, I had additional helpings along with ice cream for dessert. I was not sure if it had to do with watching my favorite baseball team "live," but on that evening, my satiety for food was non-existent. I was literally eating all night long.

Looking back at this episode of my life, I think on the possibility of having a food addiction. This is all speculation and skepticism, but I would not be surprised if I did have this problem. I just feel grateful it did not get too out of hand and that I grasped enough alternative adjustments along the way to keep things under control.

## Nutrient Density

The idea behind nutrient-dense meals and snacks is to consume food that are so ample in vitamins and minerals that it can aid the brain's electrical signals to properly function the entire body. I am not going to delve into the neurological processes of the human brain, but I will address a few commonalities about it just for the sake of contemplation. Take reference to my evening at the baseball game. My satiety went haywire when I consumed all that junk food. There was no nutritional value on all those burgers and hot dogs I was eating. What ended up occurring was me having the craving for more of that type of food. The signals were not activating the way they were supposed to.

Our brains are an astonishing internal part of our human body, and at the same time, they may be the most sensitive. It is imperative that we take care of our precious central nervous system by eating foods that promote healthy activity. Cravings for our most favorite foods will never go away, and it will be embedded in all of us due to our upbringing and the differing cultures we are exposed to. We must learn how to control those cravings and build a solid positive relationship with food. This is a tough love scenario you must impose on yourself.

In my case, I needed to take things one day at a time. Am I successful 100% of the time? No, I am not! There are times where I even need to break the day down into four-hour increments just so I can have the ease of internalizing my actions.

A trick I have learned from an acquaintance of mine who is a wellness advocate is to self-talk before deciding with nutrition. Let me elaborate with this tactic and create a common scenario. You decide to eat out and buy lunch one random workday during your lunch hour. Meal prepping was out of the question because of time constraints or there was no more food in the refrigerator. As you leave your workplace and head out, you are presented with two meal choices. Meal A is full of green leafy veggies, avocado, tomato, nuts, seeds, and a simple vinaigrette. Meal B is fried chicken wings, french fries, and a soda pop. We can easily distinguish what meal is denser with nutritional value, the question is what decision you will make at that moment.

Might I add, that moment I am putting emphasis on is a duration of maybe five to ten seconds. That single decision can sway one way or the other on how you perform and feel the rest of your work shift and then into your evening hours with your family life. Seriously contemplate this because these are common decisions we execute every day.

Remove yourself from your being and look at it from the outside in. It is as if you are having a short discussion with mindfulness. Ask yourself these questions: What will I gain from having Meal A versus Meal B? How am I going to feel if I consume Meal A versus Meal B?

Here lies the wildcard in all this: Meal A will provide better nutrition, but you can still choose Meal B. If you are okay with the circumstances and you did enough self-evaluation on your psychological talk to yourself, choose Meal B. The catch though is that you must have the correct feelings and emotions by making that other meal choice. There should not be any feelings of deprivation occurring because that is a red flag for relapse and old habits that you wanted gone when you began your health journey.

If you answered, "What will I gain from eating Meal B?" with "I will get a very indulgent meal and I am fine with it because I know

I can balance my lifestyle with this choice," and coming into those terms is good enough. The old way of approaching this scenario is of a restrictive mindset. We need to be more alert with these choice implications. Moreover, we need to put a stop on labeling food that is "good" and "bad." This is a mentality that will hinder your progress toward attaining your goals. What it all boils down to is your relationship with food, acknowledging the way you are thinking and feeling in those moments, and catching all those triggers. These tactics speak volumes on the way you see and fuel yourself with food. And remember: food is neither good nor bad, it will either fill you or fuel you.

## Convenience Over Cooking

I enjoy eating in restaurants, the experience of dining out, being in the company of friends or family, and observing how staff conduct themselves in running an establishment from their customer service and quality of cooking, and not to mention the ambience a restaurant can give to its patrons.

Most may already know this, but eating in restaurants is costly. Prices are five to ten times its original price point depending on where the restaurant is located. Owners and executive chefs must navigate and consider overhead, payroll for employee staff members, utilities, supplies, and labor when they price their food items. I recently went to a fabulous pasta restaurant that charged eighteen dollars for a great bowl of Bolognese but would have cost me about four dollars to make at home. The glass of wine ran me fifteen dollars, whereas in the grocery market, I could have purchased a whole bottle for the same price. So, you ask, what am I trying to get at here?

The point I want to home in on is we tend to choose convenience over labor, planning, and prep work. Whether you choose convenience over cooking/prep work or the other way around, something has got to give, and something must be sacrificed whether it be time, energy output, or expenses.

Earlier in the book I mentioned how the art and idea of cooking may seem trivial to many people (especially the young adults of today's generation), and it may feel like there is too much time being consumed on a craft that takes so much practice. I am here to inform you that it does not have to feel that way. And like every aspect involved with a wellness transformation, all you need to do is break it down to manageable steps and gradually get better at it as time rolls along. The process of cooking also follows the steps of "A to Z" that I alluded to earlier in the book. You have to slowly, gradually familiarize yourself from the ground up. You cannot start at "A" and expect to be an expert right away. There is no such thing as an overnight process with the idea of cooking or with anything that encompasses health transformations!

I was a hot mess during my first few years of cooking as a hobby. I made mistakes, and I learned from those mistakes along the way and picked up some tips on ergonomics and coordination around the kitchen as I worked on the craft. When you reach a certain level of cooking where you feel very confident in your skills, it makes a world of difference when you undergo a transformation. Due to all that exposure around the kitchen, the skill of cooking comes easy to me.

Cooking is an asset to have in your arsenal because you can manipulate the flavors to cater to your palate. Moreover, and most importantly, the biggest advantage you gain when you feel great about cooking is you become the sole dictator of what ingredients go into your foods. I coined the subtitle "convenience over cooking" because I feel that in today's world, some other source or person is prepping the foods we eat. It is up to us to flip the script and choose cooking over convenience.

# Chapter 12

# *Perplexing the Human Body*

*Frustration is the fertilizer of Champions.*

—*Andre Genovesi*

A couple of weeks into a results-oriented health transformation, you will feel different about yourself. In about a month, you will visually see the difference, and within about two months, others in your circle will notice the change. If you are consistent for a whole year, people will be in awe. By this point, you are into the teeth of your journey, and you are following through on your exercise regimen. A lot has already taken place with you within the three realms of your mindset, physicality, and emotions.

You have poured a lot of your efforts into fueling yourself correctly and appropriately. Then all of the sudden, out of nowhere, comes that mind block, that proverbial wall has appeared, and it feels like you have reached the plateau. We have all gone through it, and this plateau not only appears with the physical side of things but with the mental and spiritual as well. This is the point of the journey where it can feel like you have arrived at the goal weight you wanted to reach and where you can let your guard down. I am here to tell you that this part of the transformation is only the beginning.

Maintenance and adaptation continue as you keep grinding away at the lifestyle. Frustration may creep in if you let it, but there is a way around this obstacle. I mentioned in the early portion of this book that the premise behind a lifestyle is the journey, and that there is no *there*. When your vision is stretched, you will discover other ventures that you can implement to prolong your wellness progression. You will become more comfortable trying new things that may have seemed too uncomfortable for you to try before you started on the journey of health and wellness. Workout routines, supplementation, and eating patterns are meant to be altered. What I will delve into now are different things you can try if that level of frustration becomes too overwhelming for you to handle.

## The B Essential Varietals

It is so easy to get caught in a routine that feels and suits your daily schedule and family livelihood. The routine includes your exercise programs, your meal prep, and your personal me time. However, I firmly believe that the human body can sense that routine. It will know when you are going to eat, sleep, and work out. This can be a very challenging tactic to execute for many due to time constraints, but it is my firm belief that you have to mix up your routine as much as you can so you can confuse the human body. Think about it: if your body is acclimated to a routine, it will get comfortable. This will then coherently translate to you feeling comfortable emotionally.

There needs to be a transference of skills and tactics in a periodic manner so that the body never gets comfortable in a set of predictable occurrences.

It is imperative to keep pushing the envelope of varietal tactics so that you avoid sitting back into this mentality of "My job is finished." When that plateau appears, try easing up on your workload and intensity, and implement multiple low-impact activities such as walking. Avoid eating the same food on a daily/weekly basis and working out on the same timeframe on a daily/weekly basis. Variety is the spice of life. Choose different foods, eat at different times. On some occasions, intake a few extra calories to throw off your body's awareness. Indulge a bit with your favorite food and your favorite dessert. Keep in mind, this is a lifestyle (not a life sentence) for the rest of your life. Choose different exercises to partake in and execute your activities/workouts at different times of the day.

All these tactics can be considered while being mindful of food sensitivities or whether you fall under a specific dietary category (vegan, vegetarian, etc.). Change the meal prep on a weekly basis if it's feasible. Experiment with different nutrient-rich foods and switch your meat proteins up occasionally.

Keep your tastes entertained. Test out other combinations of seasonings and herb usage with your vegetables so that you break the monotony vegetables can have on you if you do the same thing over and over. Modalities with exercise is so imperative to switch up. You cannot strenuously exercise for so many days in a row; there must be a switch of intensity every now and then.

I preach these strategies because I experienced this firsthand where I was in this mentality of a constant unrelenting "go" on exercise and was repeatedly buying the same foods over and over when I made trips to the grocery store. When you approach and confront that plateau, everything seems to be settled in this lull state.

In the past, I tried to break that cycle by attempting to go harder at the gym. Then I recalled my early years where I tried to out-gym not only just nutrition but my mental obstacles also. I had to step back and remove myself from the situation and seriously soul search on how to handle this situation. When I started to implement the varietals, everything became much more at ease. I was looking forward to each new week because I would plan out the meal patterns and the exercise routines where there was a big mixture of exercises focusing on all the physical fitness components that are essential to come to terms with.

## Diets Do Not Work, You Work!

The word *must* is a powerful, driving word that will cause change no matter what type of intention you have. I will not preface the word *must* in the subcategory of this chapter but will ask to consider contemplation and acknowledgment. Have you ever noticed the first three letters in the word *diet?* What word do those letters spell? Moreover, have you ever noticed the first word that is naturally present when you think of the word *lifestyle?* Which would you rather be a part of?

From my experience, diets are difficult for me to sustain, and they are not realistic. Diets made me look at the weighing scale and how many repetitions I can do with my squats, bench presses, and pushups. I got fixated on the game of numerical statistics, which in due time, I lost interest in it because it felt arduous. Lifestyles are more of an infinite game. You have to evolve and adapt with the times, and you have to be hungry to learn more and be proactively inquisitive. The lifestyle experience was more worthwhile for me because I worked to get to that other end where I felt comfortable in my own skin, where I got rid of physical pain due to inflammation, and discovered the notion of not knowing how great I can feel, until I felt so great.

Think about this: If we were all on top of our priorities regarding wellness, execution of exercise, activity, meditation, and nutrition, would we need pharmaceuticals and a pill for every illness? Would general internal doctors even be needed? Or can we live in a world we design for ourselves where food, human movement, and efficient rest is our natural medicine and healer?

One thing is for sure, it is completely in your power to attain all of what I mentioned for yourself. You are the driving force behind this notion, you are the one that can make something that seems impossible, possible! A financial educator, a medical doctor, a life coach, entrepreneurial mentors, a wellness advocate can prescribe the strategies, but ultimately it is not about that adviser or coach.

The heroics come from you! You are the one that makes a nutritional regimen and an appropriate exercise/activity program that works! What occurs in the distant horizon is that you end up becoming that inspiration for people and become that go-to person. People will look up to you and view you as a champion! They will be aware and end up knowing that you persevered through the rough patches, adversity, and frustration to come out on the other end. Inspirational people can help you build your formula, but they are not doing this for you.

The bottom line, formulizations are determined by your actions, driving spirit, and positivity.

# Chapter 13

# *The Three We Oversee*

*Taking time to rest, renew, and refresh yourself is not wasted time. Recharge. Choose what energizes you.*

—*Melody Beattie*

So, I guess the secret is out. You have to put in the work in order for your health transformation to transpire. However, in this chapter I want to discuss three supplemental aspects that need careful attention to when you attempt transformation. I take pride in being consistent with sufficient rest, hydration, and flexibility exercises daily. These three aspects often go overlooked, and we have this tendency to gauge transformations as hard work. With that said, there is no doubt work has to be put in, but on the flip side, we all need proper principles on rejuvenation. Rest, hydration, and stretching are three principles that are underrated in my honest, humble opinion.

## Rest

As a former physical education teacher and athletics coach/ administrator, I know rest is essential for us to function in this job.

No matter how much I anticipate and prepare, the month of May always seemed to be my Achilles heel. It was like this for my other colleagues as well. It was as if our minds are already on summer vacation, but we still had a solid five weeks ahead of us to tend to.

I viewed the school year almost like an NBA basketball season. Both time periods are very similar where both entities begin and end within a similar time frame with the summer season as "time off" away from the craft. The issue I want to touch upon though is during the month of May. This is the time of the school year where teachers and administrators are the most fatigued, but yet they must be at the top of their game and putting out their best efforts. Everything that leads up to the month of May starting from August of the previous calendar year seems to go very fast, and the last five weeks of the school year feels like five months.

What I found so flabbergasting was no matter how much rest I got; my mind was always mentally drained. I went to bed exhausted from the day's work and got a solid eight to nine hours of sleep, but that all did not matter. Physically I felt recharged, but mentally, I was out on my feet. When I say, "out on my feet," it was as if I fell victim to just going through the motions of the job. It got to the point where I needed to lean upon my colleagues for assistance, and mentally, I had to break the school day down into hourly chunks and focus there. I was grateful for their leveraging, and I felt the spirit of teamwork through those times.

My other episode with rest occurred when I did my five half marathon races in eighteen months. As a reminder, this was prior to my lifestyle transformation program. As I mentioned, I was training for my half marathon that occurred in the month of June, and I remember working out at the school gym after I did a coaching session of track and field with my secondary level students. I cherished the opportunity of coaching at this school, because the people were supportive, and I had the chance to interact with other educators and coaches of different walks of life. Not to mention as well, it was along the Pacific coastline, so the weather for distance training was quite ideal.

I decided to get in a forty-five-minute circuit station workout at the school basketball gym before I headed home for the evening. I felt so good running up and down that basketball floor and performing multiple exercises that tested my endurance. I remembered this workout vividly because toward my cooldown exercise with me profusely perspiring, I felt this intuitive inkling coming over me. It was as if my consciousness was telling me to take caution and be mindful of my body. I shrugged it away and thought nothing of it after. However, if you recall, I said my body gave way in the month of April, which was two months prior to that half marathon event. Sure enough, the next morning I did a 10K running event with my family. I went into that race feeling good and well-conditioned, and then I felt a buckle on my left knee midway through the race. I did not want to believe what just happened to me, so I went on for a week in denial before I realized that the training had caught up with me.

Fast-forward to June, as I explained in the introduction, I ended up participating in that half marathon race and completed it with a hampered left leg. It was a very proud moment, but I knew going forward my days of competing in long-distance races were over. I had to explore and discover a new outlet of my exercise regimen, and I did not know how to do that.

The lesson I learned in all of this stemmed back to the notion of rest. No matter how much I rested and recuperated from those eighteen months of running, I felt that my body could not recover. I felt worn out and sluggish even after solid nights of rest. Nowadays, with a different perspective on exercise and activity, I listen and rely heavily on my intuitions with regard to exertion and the types of exercises I partake in. If my mind says *go* and my body is telling me *no*, I will make that final decision and forgo a workout for that day because of what my body is telling me.

I am no longer in that state of "no pain no gain." There is no shame whatsoever in taking time for yourself and resting so you can be better the next day. There is this stigma of being weak because you need rest. No! There is nothing wrong with taking time to reset your mind, body, and soul. Home into your circadian rhythm, feel it, and listen to it!

## Stretching

Along with the daily thirty minutes of physical activity and periodic forty-five-to-sixty-minute workout sessions, I incorporate and dedicate a full hour of stretching every day of the calendar year. Stretching is another underrated notion that not a lot of people take into consideration. This is another nonnegotiable to me. This characteristic is embedded in my life because I know how I am going to feel after I do a solid stretch session.

Now you will ask yourself, "Do I have to do sixty minutes a day every day?" The answer is, no, you do not have to. Quite frankly, it took me probably a full decade before I committed to doing sixty minutes of stretching a day. I started out by just doing ten to fifteen minutes per day, and I slowly made that a habit. As time went on, the pattern naturally developed and manifested. The habit became a behavior, and then the behavior became second nature, like a reflex.

Like with everything that starts off new, you will have to build and leverage the skills you know and then refine over time. Why stretching? What is the purpose of devoting time to do these static movements? I can tell you from experience, not only does flexibility improve your mobility, but it also stimulates everything from your mind clarity and your composure. An appreciation of your body performance and functioning increases as you get consistent with stretching. In addition, discovering a body that will support everything you do is truly astonishing.

With these factors addressed, stretching has a complimenting sidekick. Stretching's number one partner is water hydration.

## Water Hydration

Water consumption is the most simplistic practice to enhancing vitality. How much water is enough water? Typically, you want to consume half your body weight in ounces. However, those numbers can change in an increasing manner, depending on how physically active you are. When there are days I am not feeling up for a workout, I can always revert to stretching and hydration. Think about it. Stretching and basic yoga poses to strengthen your core can count as physical activity. If you're feeling in a rut, these two practical wellness disciplines can serve as a foundation to set you up appropriately if you decide to ramp up and reset your exercise program.

There are myriad benefits if you become consistent with water hydration. I will not list them all, but just be mindful that water is your best ally when it comes to transforming your body. It serves as a regulator and aids blood flow to your essential organs and muscles. Moreover, water should be the only form of liquid anyone should be drinking. I advise to never ever drink your calories! With the few exceptions of the occasional glass of wine or pint of beer during special life moments.

Some common practices I adhere to regarding this discipline all stem back to meal prepping. Along with the food I prepare and cook for an upcoming work week, I also prep my water every evening before the following day. This may or may not work to your advantage, but I will share a strategy that has done wonders for me.

Along with your prepped meals and snacks, I recommend bringing three water thermos/tumblers with you to your occupation. Dependent on the nature of the job and its conduciveness, preferably you would always want one water thermos with you, one in the lounge room refrigerator (assuming there is a lounge room for breaks), and one thermos inside your car. The idea with this tactic is that no matter where you go during your day at work, water is always ready and available with you at any time and at any locale.

No matter what field you're in, I strongly urge you to keep drinking water available in your vehicle because some jobs call for the individual to commute to multiple locations. You can bring one thermos to ease the load but think twice about this. You would always have to refill your container if you are adamant on your hydration. If you get good about keeping track of your three water containers, you rarely have to make trips to the break room to refill. This will not only save you time and money, but it poses a huge convenience on your behalf because you already prepped the hydration strategy the evening before.

Another tip that may work for you is bringing one big flask of water that will hold approximately sixty-five to seventy ounces of water (give or take). I have even seen the 128-ounce plastic container, which is equivalent to the full gallon and has time reminder markers on the bottle itself. If this option is chosen, you have extra visual accountability to keep pace with the gallon intake. This is a very effective strategy, but the big jug does not work for how I like to function. There are drawbacks, pros, and cons to each of these hydration practices. The challenge is to just commit to the process and know the benefits of consistent, proper hydration.

**Water Hacks:** Water is an essential beverage, but let's face it, it can get boring sometimes. Below are tips to spruce up your water experience. You can add your own ingredients to match your preferences. These water alternatives are just to give you ideas, and in addition to that, once you find the ingredients that best go with your taste palate, the more you will consume water so you can either meet that one gallon a day or your required fluid ounces.

**Mojito H20** (my personal favorite): mint, lime wedges, cucumber

**Nature's Sprite:** lemon and lime wedges

**Citrus Berry Combo:** raspberry/lime, strawberry/lemon, blackberry/blueberry/Meyer lemon

**Peels:** orange peel, grapefruit peel, flat leaf Italian parsley

# Chapter 14

# *The Physical Fitness Components*

*Physical fitness is not only one of the most important keys to a healthy body, it is the basis of dynamic and creative intellectual activity.*

—*John F. Kennedy*

## The Five Physical Fitness Components:

1. Flexibility
2. Muscular Endurance
3. Muscular Strength
4. Cardiorespiratory Fitness
5. Body Composition

In the previous chapters, I mentioned that I taught physical education to kids age five to thirteen. I took pride in what I did as a movement educator because I felt I exposed students to diverse activities, games, locomotor skills, and exercises. I used the subject matter to build an emotional connection with my students so they could turn to me for support and guidance. I was not the PE teacher that rolled the ball out and told the students to go play and stay out of trouble. I was the one who provided structure and a set of boundaries so everyone could engage in the activities in a proper manner. I was the teacher who gave constructive feedback and praise throughout the activity duration.

This time in my life served as a propeller to what I underwent in my own transformation. The teachings led me to explore within myself, taught me lessons on how to interact with young children, and opened new horizons in wellness. My PE program put a lot of emphasis on a variety of movement skills along with the ability to communicate positively during games. I went beyond the threshold of recreational games, and I taught my students the importance of being active and being consistent with the art and science involved with movement.

But the most important trait I emphasized as a teacher was communicating the importance to care for your body, by means of food nourishment and injury prevention. It was so rewarding to witness development and progression with students' performance. I felt so humbled and proud that I had a small role in their overall growth.

## Secondary Students

When I first implemented the physical fitness components into my PE curriculum for students grades six to eight, I methodically communicated to my students why I was doing this and how it would benefit them in the future. I intently told them that the five physical fitness components were implemented not only for the sake of testing and giving them written assessments. The main purpose was for exploring self-education because at some point in time, what is going to matter for them is their own health and the values that revolve around it. Most importantly, it is the implementation of their own personal standards to affect how they view and feel about wellness.

I received some mixed reactions and feelings. At the time, a good number of students did not see it my way, and I got some pushback from parents because they viewed PE as a class of recreation and "play time." There were other sets of parents on the other side of the spectrum who were thrilled that I was going over these aspects to help their children throughout their lives in the realm of health and wellness. Regardless of the skepticism, I pushed forward on what I believed was right, and what I believe is the knowledge I can pass to these students as they got older.

Over time, I added musculoskeletal foundations. To accompany the fitness components, my students had to familiarize themselves with a total of forty-four bones and muscles. The most rewarding part of teaching students these concepts happened after they left the private school I was teaching at. A few of them came back to thank me on going over those components and the muscles/bones diagram because they had a head start on what was already taught to them in their junior high years.

Looking back at my teachings, I did not realize until later that I gradually became a better advocate of health, better teacher on effective living, and a more diverse athlete.

# Empathy

The main reason I elaborated on my teaching experience is because the profession made me into a person of empathy. Empathy supersedes and outweighs personal ego. Ego is a good thing to have, but there is a fine line between having that confidence in abilities and then being viewed as an arrogant showboat. Being empathetic anchors down that ego and places it on hold and keeps it concealed.

With the case of prospecting and mentoring others who want to improve their well-being, consultants and coaches must have the ability to empathize. My prior educational experience made it accessible for me to practice empathy because I knew how it functions and how it is a vital role in relaying communication and prospecting clients. I have the great blessed ability to feel the other person's emotion and body language. I am not stating I am perfect with this ability, but for the most part, I have a deep trust with my gut instinct and what my intuitions communicate to me. As a teacher, the number one priority to be able to execute is placing yourself in the shoes of the student and feeling out the emotions of what they are going through. Building that important rapport between teacher and student was always on my mind, and it made me take consideration of different likes and dislikes students have.

This holds true for me today with my current job and side gig as a wellness consultant. Forming that trust, bond, and respect means everything when helping someone go through a health transformation journey. Empathy opens the door to another virtue that is true to my heart and something that I am still improving upon, and that valuable virtue is tolerance.

## Tolerance

Tolerance is easy when everything is going well. I tend to be tolerant when it is just me in control of whatever task, duty, or challenge is thrown at me and how I progress through those battles. When the variables around a situation are thrown on a loop though, that is when my tolerance is challenged and I would have to pause, take some deep, meaningful breaths, and consciously talk myself into having patience. When other people are involved in these scenarios, I have to remind myself that not everyone will work up to my capacity and expectations.

Regarding teacher-student relationships, empathy will definitely lead you to being patient with the students, especially if they have learning disabilities. Tolerance is tested when defiance comes into play. Defiance can occur easily with students, not to mention colleagues as well.

These types of scenarios I am explaining can also correspond to life coaches and wellness consultants working with their clients. I have witnessed many breakdowns and breakthroughs from my former students. I have also experienced my own breakdowns and breakthroughs that I had to deal with and figure out. Neither I nor my students could have handled those trying times successfully if we did not have persistence on our side.

# Part III Implementation:
# *Food Recipes and Activity Ideas*

Part III of the book touched upon the physical side of the process and has much to do with active execution that is stimulated by your mindset and the vigor of your spiritual soul. You truly have to come from a place of intentional desire and wants. The drive of your work ethic has to come from within. There are so many interpretations to that statement; you will need to discover your own. The following recipes and activities are things that have worked for me because I know exactly how I am going to feel after I consume and execute.

## The Hulk Salad

I named this salad after the Marvel superhero because of the green vegetables in this dish. There are many variations to this spectacularly nutrient-dense meal. I mentioned before how you have to make vegetables exciting in Chapter 11. This is one way to do just that— have a variety of cooking techniques to slightly alter the taste of the veggies as they hit your palate.

The Hulk salad has a foundational base of a lemon vinaigrette, kale, arugula, carrots, and avocado. Those five elements are the core to this dish that I do not change. It is the other vegetables I put in for variety. I will share two renditions of this salad. This is a salad I consume during my work shift. I feel invigorated after ten minutes of consuming this salad, and I follow up the meal with a five-minute walk around my workplace to aid digestion. Give this a try sometime and you should notice a big difference in the second portion of your shift.

The Hulk Salad #1:

Kale

Arugula

Lemon vinaigrette (recipe to follow)

Julienne carrots

Sliced avocado

Toasted sunflower seeds

Roasted cauliflower

Sun-dried tomato

The Hulk Salad #2:

Kale

Arugula

Lemon vinaigrette (recipe to follow)

Julienne carrots

Slice avocado

Steamed broccoli

Hemp seeds

Nutritional yeast

Toasted pepitas

Roma tomato

Procedures:

***Lemon vinaigrette:*** Slice two wedges of lemon, squeeze juice into a bowl. Do a two-count extra virgin olive oil pour with the lemon juice. Stir vigorously for twenty seconds, set aside.

***Roasted veggies:*** Preheat oven at 425 degrees, place veggies on a sheet pan coated in olive oil and seasoned with salt and pepper. Roast for 20 minutes, flipping the veggies at the halfway point (10th minute). Set aside.

***Steamed broccoli:*** On a strained double boiler, fill the bottom pot with water and bring to a rolling boil. Place the sliced broccoli inside on the strainer pot above the boiler pot and steam for 5 to 6 minutes. Set aside.

Salad Preparation:

1. Pour the vinaigrette along the side walls of a salad bowl.
2. Gather all the vegetable ingredients and pre-slice them ahead of time so that everything is set to go.
3. Except for the sliced avocado, place all veggies inside the salad bowl.
4. Toss and flip the salad so the vinaigrette coats the ingredients.
5. Top the salad with the slice avocado.

## The 24 & 24

This is a straightforward flexibility activity I incorporate into my life as much as possible. The equipment needed is a yoga mat and a twenty-four-ounce water bottle. It is simply twenty-four ounces of water to accompany twenty-four minutes of stretching. Consume the water at your own discretion. I preferably drink the water every six minutes for consistency through the activity.

The first twelve minutes of this activity is pure static stretching of the major muscles of the body (latissimus dorsi, gastrocnemius, hamstrings, quadriceps to name a few).

The second half of the exercise, I tend to execute the most basic of yoga poses such as wall sits, child poses, tree poses, high and low plank poses, and downward dog. I will hold each pose for either twenty-four seconds or twenty-four breaths. This half of the activity focuses on a healthy posture. Many occupations out there in our world are "desk jobs," and it requires people sitting in front of a computer. Posture exercises are imperative to maintain your body's ability to function at your workplace.

I will reiterate again: you do not have to follow this format. You can choose to do different mobile exercises to suit your needs. This is just to get an idea out there to help jumpstart a structured routine for yourself.

You will find more food recipes and exercise ideas in my Connect With Me & Free Resources section at the conclusion of this book.

# Chapter 15

## *Recapitulation*

*People need to be reminded more often than they need to be instructed.*
—*Samuel Johnson*

All three components of the mental, spiritual, and physical are so essential to attaining a healthy, well-balanced lifestyle and achieving the ultimate formula of *you*. With that mentioned, we need to always remember that everything stems back to our minds. Our minds feed what the soul needs with healthy, pattern-forming habits that become part of our routine.

## Part I: Mentality Recap

Attaining a proper mindset, perception, preparational skills, and reception of feedback was touched upon in Part I. We spoke about how we give with abundance to other people, but the main person that we should be giving and caring for is you. If you are not at your best internally and externally, then how can we be our best for others? Therefore, there has to be a level of selfishness on our behalf and a sense of compromise and sacrifice to take time to care for ourselves.

Focus your energy to what really matters for a transformation to occur. It is not about how you look, but rather it is about the vibes, intuition, and the feelings you have. People do not know the story behind the glory of your transformation, and they only view it from the surface. What really goes on is how you rewired your thinking and the discipline you followed so that you are not always dependent on outside factors. It is about your inner relationship with yourself and how you treat other people.

Prioritization is the linking puzzle piece within my strategies behind preparation and time management. The main idea expressed here was that preparation may feel uncomfortable at first, but as you build upon the repetitiveness of that craft, over time it will get manageable. Within preparation, we delved into the notion of meal prepping and how much more time and money can be saved if this discipline is consistently implemented. Time is our most precious commodity, and we either waste and wallow it away or we can fill our twenty-four hours with fulfillment and production. The harsh reality with time is we fill it with what feels important to us, but in order for that specific health change to occur, we have to soul-search. Reprioritize not only what is needed but what is wanted on your end. "I don't have time" is an excuse to avoid change and refute those hard confrontations along the way to reach that change.

# Part II: Spirituality & Emotions Recap

Our emotions are the core to our spirituality. Within this space, we ventured into the relevance of creating vindictive intentions, the people that impact our lives, how every body type differs from one another, and that aging is a splendid blessing. Intentions are always on a constant creation and recreation. We need them so that everything that revolves the healthy living lifestyle is pre-calculated and pre-determined. We develop our meal planning and exercise routines with a great sense of purpose so there are no surprises when we attain the results we expectedly deserve. We addressed how the people in our lives are a contributing factor on how the inner spirit can either be negatively or positively affected. They can also make or break your way of thinking and reacting. In a nutshell, we need to find people who are like minded and will link to our ultimate dreams and goals, and consequently, negate the ones who are toxic.

I want to make a final note on comparisons when it comes to witnessing different body images and body types. Be mindful, anyone and everyone that endures a transformation will see and feel different results and breakthroughs at different stages. The rate is not the same for everyone. If someone else is going at a more efficient rate of progression, instead of comparing your results to them, try looking at it as a source of inspiration or as a resource for reference. Think about it, if you have jealous feelings, there may be some bitter emotions and envy that will string along to add more uneasiness. That small adjustment on your perception of others' transformation can feed positivity to your emotions.

The last chapter on spirituality touched on aging. Here are two facts no one will ever disagree upon: at some point we are going to leave this planet, and getting older is inevitable. Your age is simply a numerical figure and you can stay youthful if you are willing to be in a state of prosperity. God willing, I plan to be around for a very long time. Not everyone on this planet gets to experience aging. Please remember, you are older, not old!

## Part III: Physical Recap

Much of the physical elements addressed in Part III revolved around the regimen you can develop on nutrition and exercise. Activity and exercise were discussed and they differ. Activity is a nonnegotiable aspect we all must execute on the daily. I proposed thirty minutes per day every day, but anyone can exceed that time limit if they wish to. Whereas in exercise, it is more concentrated and strenuous whether you are doing cardio or weight resistance training. As opposed to doing activity daily, keep exercise at a frequency of at least three times a week.

Intensity and frequency are the cogs to exercise. I like to think of them as the transmission and engine of an automobile. As you develop an exercise regimen that you feel is manageable in the beginning, you can build more exercises and implement refined movements in each. The frequency of your regimen will naturally lead to how consistent you become with the routines. I cannot stress enough to only handle as much as you can in the beginning stages, because too much too soon can lead you to quitting your journey.

Intensity defines how hard you are working within exercises and workout periods. The notion I wanted to concentrate on is the issue of familiarization of movement before you increase intensity. I always urge beginners to train as if you are in physical rehabilitation. It coerces the client/athlete to feel out the movements in a gradual manner before going full extension or full speed. Two things that occur if you focus this way: (1) your movement technique on the long run will be very good, and (2) you will build a tendency to not get injured.

As mentioned before, for performance and athleticism to work, you need to fuel your body properly with nutrient-dense food. The idea behind food as fuel is that it's so ample in vitamins and minerals that it can aid the brain's functioning so that the body does not have to work as hard with metabolization. This will have you feeling better and performing with high energy on your daily duties.

Within the realm of food comes the decisions you will have to make when it comes to choosing and planning out meals. You will come across times where you have to choose between a meal that will make you feel better and a meal that is indulgent and will taste great on your palate but will lack the nutrient density. The strategy mentioned here was to remove yourself from the situation as if you are having a conversation with yourself. "What will I get out of this meal if I choose to eat it? How am I going to feel after I have it?" The component that ties in with food and exercise is variety and the spice of life.

On the latter chapters we addressed how to mix up and have a wide variety of foods to break up the monotony that may enter your life and cause you to get frustrated and bored with the routines. The same thing goes with exercise and activity; you would want a wide range of activities, so you do not lose interest and take the gift of movement for granted. Find people who like certain types of foods and activities, so you build relationships and share common interests with each other. This is a huge advantage because you can learn from one another and help each other progress toward a common goal.

Another aspect that was addressed with food and exercise is mealtimes and workout sessions being executed at different time intervals. The body will recognize and feel a routine if it's executed consistently. If it knows you are working out and eating at the same times, it may get complacent, plateau, and then put your progression on a standstill. Hence, we are back to addressing the issue of variety. Try working out at different times of the day, especially late in the evening (although that may not work for some, it did for me). When you wake up, keep the morning routine consistent, but try to change the times of meals/snacks and the times when you execute workouts/activity.

Last, I posted for consideration purposes the five fitness components. Having the basic understanding of those components will be helpful for you because you can implement them anytime you are working out for yourself or if you are helping someone comprehend the meaning behind them through their journey. I reflected on how I taught these components to junior high students.

What it taught me on the back end was how to be an effective person of empathy.

I got into teaching physical education because I was the chubby kid who was out of shape. When I saw a student struggling, I related to those feelings and felt the need to lend a hand for them. Having the ability to step into the shoes of another person's feelings is golden when it comes to coaching and consulting. Nowadays, my empathy for consulting wellness to prospects and clients has gotten stronger. It has never wavered since I acquired that trait back when I was teaching and coaching young students, and I have so much gratitude for going through that experience because it has molded me into the wellness health advocate I am today.

## Final Thoughts

Every aspect that encompasses transformations take time to develop. There has to be a sense of tolerance around the journey of your new self. If we break down the words *transition* and *transformation*, we discover the meanings behind them and how they will aid us. *Trans* means to move across, within, and to go beyond. *Form* means to give way to a life that is brand new. Transition is where a change is happening, but something has to be let go and to succumb to an action of grieving what was. We cannot go beyond until we come to terms with our traumatic experience or hardship with health.

Transitions stem from how we think and interpret. It is imperative that we meet our shortcomings and confront them head-on to be open minded and take ownership of our vulnerabilities. It is never

ever too late to make a lifestyle adjustment, and you are never too old! Your age has nothing to do with how you show up for yourself, how you inspire, how you honor the commitments you make to yourself, or how you deal with adversity. Free yourself from the idea of body image and body shape and embrace how you can best function with the body you have. Free yourself from the societal notion of labeling food as "good" or "bad!" It is neither one or the other! Food is an asset we need in order for progression to occur. Food's purpose is to provide nourishment and energy, yet at the same time we need to keep in mind the quality of food we consume.

Vibrant vitality and positive mentality over external images and limiting beliefs every time. You either quit or keep going; both will hurt. Choose your hurt! Just know, if you choose to quit, regret may sink in, and that is another level and category of hurt you will have to come to terms with along with the physical hurt of an unhealthy body. The unhealthy route has multi-dimensional levels of hurt; the healthy route has a more manageable type of hurt.

Would you rather go through a challenging life with a body that is internally and externally out of shape or a body that is optimized all around and fully functional? We all know the answer to that question, but is there enough fortitude in us to follow through on the strategies addressed in this book?

Remember Coach Riley's quote on commitment? You are either completely all in or out, there is no in between. With that quote mentioned again, I will make a final statement to ponder on, which many may not like. In my heart of hearts, health and wellness either get worse or better as we move along the infinite game of life. There is no such thing as health and wellness tapering off and leveling out flat. Think of it as your heart going into flatline; what happens to you when you flatline? With a solid heartbeat, there is a reading on the monitor that goes up and down, just like how it is in life. You will need the hunger, the excitement, and the yearning to always practice the craft of an optimized lifestyle.

In the end, all that is going to matter is taking that next meaningful breath. Being unhealthy or healthy is going to be hard. Choose your hard!

# Connect With Me & Free Resources

As mentioned, there is no such thing as a final destination with health and wellness. There is only the journey and the willingness to adapt, grow, and learn. Let's keep the ideas, strategies, and challenges going and connect with me on social media at @brandon_adalid_

Access additional Formulation YOU resources
here for added material
to guide you along on your wellness journey.

# Acknowledgments

It truly takes a village to fully develop an individual to what they want to be in life and to take notice of their purpose in this world. The following individuals who have influenced and supported me throughout my life journey are exemplary people in their own right. I think so highly of them for their profound impact on me, and together we look forward to continual growth, health, and prosperity. Warm, sincere thoughts, deepest appreciation, and thanks go to:

My Core Four: my parents, Rudy, and Mila, and my two younger sisters, Joanne, and Christine. Your support, nourishing spirits, generosity, and love mean everything to me.

To my great friend, dedicated school educator, and science department chair Michael Flores for always standing by my side.

To my accountability partner Marco Filardi for your confidence, energy, and bright shining light.

To Daniel Sala$, keep on dancing, keep on singing! Your astonishing vibe for life is incredible and for keeping that last letter S for monetary savings.

To Joe Donato who'll always have the better smile, thicker beard, and taller height.

To my coworker and grocery section partner Alistair Watt for all the book-reading conversations and book recommendations. It is indeed a never-ending process of learning and vocabulary exposure.

To my former middle school classmate Sabrina Benjamins for your kindness, your exemplary attitude, and love.

To my former colleague, boss, and educational mentor Margaret "Peggy" Hill. I am so grateful for my affiliation with you. You are like a second mother to me.

A salute to my book coach, book mentor, "The Book Mamba" Jake Kelfer, chief elevating officer of the BIB Program. Thank you for your tireless efforts!

To my book adviser and fellow author Joe Van Geison, always reminding us to enjoy the grind.

To my entrepreneurial mentors Melissa Henault, Gustavo Bonini, and Andre Genovesi. All three of you have an amazing drive, passion, and enthusiasm for life. Your leadership development to spread among others is bar none, second to none! You three are the best at what you do!

To all my fellow dedicated authors from the March 2023 BIB Live program, Kristina Hudson, Micah Lucie, Ralph Bessard, Alexis Teichmiller, you all are terrific people.

To all my health transformation partners who are inspiring others in their inner circle of people, whom I will mention one by one because they deserve the spotlight! Big shoutouts to my sponsoring wellness coach Christine Manukyan, Reginald Jackson Sr. (because there is a junior), Tami Schiltz, Tammy List, Dana "The Man of Steele", Mike Doran, Pam de Minico Nyatsambo, Lauren Mascolo, Crystal Willis, and two of our fitness grand champions Kim Nase and Drew Putnam. You all attain a zest for life, and each one of you is amazing!

To my "Formulation YOU" Facebook page followers for your enduring everlasting support throughout this journey. This is a special group of former teammates, colleagues, classmates, and business partners. Much love and gratefulness to Arniel Brown, Cheryl Moore, Yael Moldovan, Steven Flores, Coach Terry Smith-Harris, Nina Terry, Carissa Nietschmann, Kris Mari Mosqueda, Stacey Matsuoka, Charles Yenokyan, Sandy Spangler, Lily Spangler, Wendy Mittlebach, Cindy Reitzenstein, Kimberley Lunn Dehn, Alexandria Lopez, Sharon Baires, Lynn Carnavaciolo, James Mariano, Kim Palkovic, Colleen Joyce, Brandon Salazar, Ray Vasquez, Ania Jonca, Margaret Gomez, Karla Perez Hutchinson, Karen Shea, Jenny Cee, Lisa Guzman, Steven Herzfeld, and last but not least, my fellow authors from the BIB program, Claire Sparrow, Stacy Mickelson, Kelly J Welch, Rachel Newman, and Brian Hendricks.

To my expert editor, my cover designer, and formatter for making my book come to life.

Much appreciation to the 1,500+ people I have been affiliated with, representing the communities of St. Bernardine School (Woodland Hills, CA), St. Matthews School (Pacific Palisades, CA),

Beverly Vista School (Beverly Hills, CA), St. Rose of Lima School (Simi Valley, CA), and Whole Foods Market (Glendale, CA).

All the love to my current grocery crew member family at Trader Joe's store location #252! Your accompaniment, cheerfulness, and laughter mean so much to me.

To Tara Garrison: physical fitness trainer, holistic wellness coach, and author in the health and wellness space. I appreciate the fact that we share a like-mindedness to our philosophies. You are an inspirational figure in the world of healing, love, fitness, and nutrition. I cannot say enough great things about you.

To YOU! I am so thankful for you taking the time, investment, and space to read my book and hear out my personal story. I am grateful for your support and acknowledgment, and I'm hoping that the book made some kind of influential positive impact on your life.

To my health transformation business mentors Amanda Edwards Hamm, and Renee Bass Schreibman for your endless love, support, and tutelage.

My great friends Rebbeca Douglas, David Hamm, Jayson Mallari, and Omar Ojeda. Outside of my own family, you four are important, prominent figures in my life.

And last, to Cammie Tolleshaug. You are an exceptional talent! Much love to you for reviving my beliefs and my soul.

# About the Author

Brandon Adalid is a dedicated wellness consultant and dynamic health speaker. He is a former physical education teacher and athletics coach and attains a high passion for health advocacy for the people affiliated with him. After fifteen years in education, Brandon got involved in the grocery industry. He currently sets high standards for himself the past few years as a grocery crew member and takes pride in his work. Brandon truly understands the gift of movement and does not take that blessing for granted. He enjoys setting the example for everyone to truly step into their power of mindfulness and health. His role as a wellness consultant adds to his credibility as a contributor to his purpose. He works diligently to promote a positive self-image with his clients and has a strong personal and professional character. Brandon enjoys sharing his ideas on what it takes to eat, live, and perform at the healthiest way possible so others can feel their best selves for the time they have on this planet too.

Brandon currently resides in Southern CA, approximately fifteen miles north of Los Angeles. When Brandon is not at the grocery store or consulting wellness tactics to his prospects, you will find him in the culinary kitchen testing out new (and old) recipes and finding more nutrient-dense food combinations he can share.

www.ingramcontent.com/pod-product-compliance
Lightning Source LLC
Chambersburg PA
CBHW070716130626
46553CB00005B/2020